Permutation and Randomization Tests for Trading System Development Algorithms in C++

Third Edition

Timothy Masters

Great effort has been undertaken in ensuring that the content of this book, including all associated computer code, is as close to correct as possible. However, errors and omissions are inevitable in a work of this extent; they are surely present. Neither this book nor the associated computer code are meant as professional advice. No guarantee is made that this material is free of errors and omissions, and the reader assumes full liability for any losses associated with use of this material. The algorithms described in this book and implemented in the associated programs are experimental and not vetted by any outside experts or tested in the crucible of time. Please treat them accordingly.

About the author:

Timothy Masters received a PhD in mathematical statistics with a specialization in numerical computing. Since then he has continuously worked as an independent consultant for government and industry. His early research involved automated feature detection in high-altitude photographs while he developed applications for flood and drought prediction, detection of hidden missile silos, and identification of threatening military vehicles. Later he worked with medical researchers in the development of computer algorithms for distinguishing between benign and malignant cells in needle biopsies. For the last twenty years he has focused primarily on methods for evaluating automated financial market trading systems. He has authored twelve books on practical applications of predictive modeling:

Practical Neural Network Recipes in C++ (Academic Press, 1993)
Signal and Image Processing with Neural Networks (Wiley, 1994)
Advanced Algorithms for Neural Networks (Wiley, 1995)
Neural, Novel, and Hybrid Algorithms for Time Series Prediction (Wiley, 1995)
Assessing and Improving Prediction and Classification (Apress, 2018)
Deep Belief Nets in C++ and CUDA C: Volume I: Restricted Boltzmann Machines and Supervised Feedforward Networks (Apress, 2018)
Deep Belief Nets in C++ and CUDA C: Volume II: Autoencoding in the Complex Domain (Apress, 2018)
Deep Belief Nets in C++ and CUDA C: Volume III: Convolutional Nets (Apress, 2018)
Data Mining Algorithms in C++ (Apress, 2018)
Testing and Tuning Market Trading Systems (Apress, 2018)
Extracting and Selecting Features for Data Mining (Create Space, 2019)
Statistically Sound Indicators for Financial Market Prediction: Algorithms in C++ (KDP, 2019)

The software referenced in this text may be downloaded from the author's website:
TimothyMasters.info

Contents

Contents

1

Introduction

A Simple Motivational Example

Suppose you manage a trading firm or other financial institution, and a person comes to you looking for a job. She presents a fairly impressive item on her resume: over the last year, shortly before the close of the market every day she decided to be long, short, or out of the market through the next day. If she chose to be in the market, she would immediately open a position and then close it just before the market close the following day. After placing her daily decisions in a spreadsheet alongside the daily returns, you do some simple math. For every day when she said to be long you add that day's return to a running sum. For every day she wanted to be short you subtract that day's return. This simple math shows that she enjoyed a notable net profit.

Unfortunately, you were not planning to hire someone right now, so you need to be quite sure that her performance was outstanding before bringing her into the firm. What if she was just lucky? It happens. Or what if the market was in a strong up-trend over the year and she chose to be long most of the time? Some evaluation philosophies say that this is just being smart, but you favor the philosophy that drifting with the tide is no big deal; a great trader *outperforms* the tide. You would prefer that test.

Hypothesis Tests

So how do you judge her performance, beyond by just looking at her equity curve and making an intuitive decision? The standard way of handling a problem like this is with a *hypothesis test*. If you are totally unfamiliar with this concept, you should consult any Statistics 101 textbook. But the general idea is that we specify a *null hypothesis*, which in this and most other problem domains is the situation of "whatever we are testing is worthless." Then we compute the probability, called a *p-value*, that if the null hypothesis is true (the thing tested is worthless) we could have gotten results at least as good as we obtained. If we find that this probability is small then we conclude that the null hypothesis is probably false, and we rule in favor of the *alternative hypothesis*. In other words, we conclude that the thing being tested truly is good.

Several possibilities for making the hiring decision now come to mind:

- Perform an ordinary Student's t-test on the daily returns. Compute the probability (p-value) that her mean daily return could have been as large as it was if the true expected value of her daily returns was zero or less (the null hypothesis of worthlessness. We can immediately write off this approach, because market returns are notoriously non-normal, and the t-test is sensitive to this. Even a single wild return, win or loss, would totally invalidate this test. And it has another problem as well, mentioned in the next point.

- Perform a bootstrap test of the same null hypothesis. This largely solves the problem of non-normality, as bootstraps are much more robust against outliers than the t-test. But we agreed earlier that your criterion for excellence would preferably be that she *outperform* the tide of a rising market. Testing a null hypothesis that the true mean return is less than or equal to zero does not fill the bill, because just unintelligently floating with the tide will produce a positive return that may well produce a small p-value.

- Compute the expected mean daily return of a random system having the same number of long and short positions as your job candidate had. This is easy; just compute the fraction of time the system is long, subtract the fraction of time it is short, and multiply by the net change over the entire market history tested. Then perform a bootstrap test of the null hypothesis that the expected returns from her trading system are less than or equal to the computed expected random return. This is actually a pretty good test in regard to mean daily returns outperforming the tide of the trend. However, if you want to evaluate some other performance measure such as a risk-adjusted return (Sharpe ratio, Ulcer Index, etc.) this will not do. Bootstrap tests are notoriously poor when evaluating statistics with a long right tail, which you often have with risk-adjusted performance measures. The Sharpe ratio bootstraps particularly poorly, and any measure involving order, such as drawdown, is totally invalid for a bootstrap test.

Overview of the Monte-Carlo Permutation Test

None of the options just shown are very good if you are concerned with *outperforming* the tide, but all is not lost. We have an excellent alternative, the *Monte-Carlo permutation test* (*MCPT*). This test makes no distribution assumptions, is rugged against outliers, automatically evaluates performance above and beyond riding with the trend, and can be used with nearly any measure of performance, even those involving order.

The key to understanding the Monte-Carlo permutation tests presented in this book is to know that they always involve order in some form, often in the context of pairing. In the example under discussion, the job applicant has provided an ordered series of long/short/neutral positions, and these are paired with similarly ordered daily market returns. Each day we have a decision about the position for that day (made the prior afternoon) paired with the market return for that day. Our null hypothesis is that the applicant's pairings are effectively random, not related to the market returns in any useful manner. If her returns are sufficiently good we will obtain a small p-value and thereby favor the alternative hypothesis, that her pairing of positions with next-day returns was intelligent.

To be clear, this particular example involves pairing of ordered series. We are hoping to see evidence that the job applicant's pairing of positions with next-day returns is intelligent, providing unusually good performance. But having 'good' performance is not enough. Before we hire this person we want to be reasonably sure that her decisions were intelligent, not just lucky. Intuition provides a quick-and-dirty way to test this question: we destroy her pairing by permuting either her decision series or the day-return series (they are equivalent, of course) and compute the performance obtained by this random pairing. If her pairing was intelligent, we would expect her performance to exceed that obtained by random pairing.

Suppose we do this and find that, indeed, randomizing the pairing decreases the performance. She wins this little contest. That's great, right? She beat the randomized pairing. Hire her.

But wait. Not so fast. Suppose her trade decisions were truly worthless, effectively random. She'd be on par with any other random pairing, and hence there is a 50-50 chance that she'd win anyway. We sure shouldn't base an important hiring decision on a 'favorable' outcome that had a probability of 0.5 of happening even if her decisions were worthless.

Maybe we'd better try some more randomizations and see how she stacks up against them. Suppose we do 9 randomizations, computing a performance score for each, and suppose she beats them all. That's a slam-dunk, right? Almost, but we need to be more rigorous. Here's a thought experiment. Get ten slips of paper. Write her score on one and write the nine random scores on the other nine slips. Now lay them out on the table, sorted from lowest performance to highest. Suppose her choices were worthless, essentially random. Then all ten of these performances are on par with one another, and hence all orders of performance are equally likely. The applicant's slip of paper could land in any of the ten sorted positions with equal probability. In particular, she could land in the coveted best slot with probability 1/10=0.1. She could land in either that slot or the second-best with probability 2/10=0.2, and so forth. We see that even if she beat all nine randomized trials she would still have a one-in-ten chance of being the best performer, even if her decisions were worthless. This is good, but not really the slam-dunk we thought it might be.

We can make this process still more rigorous. Suppose we do m randomizations. Then, if the thing we are testing (intelligent pairing of position and return in this example) is truly worthless, there is a probability of $(k+1)/(m+1)$ that k of them have a performance at least as good as that of the original, non-randomized performance. In our current example, in which we do nine randomizations of the applicant's pairing with next-day returns, there is a probability of $(0+1)/(9+1)=0.1$ that none of the randomized scores will be at least as good as hers. She beat them all. And there is a probability of 0.2 that she will come in at least second-best, and so forth.

Thus we see that it is in our best interest to perform as many random permutations as possible, because this will make the denominator $m+1$ as large as possible. In this way, we make beating the randomized scores very difficult if the thing being tested is truly worthless. The smaller the computed probability, the more confident we can be in the quality of the thing being tested, and we can get small probabilities only with large m.

In order to satisfy statistical purists, I should briefly mention a subtle point about hypothesis tests of the sort I just described. At the risk of being skewered, I'll assert that in my opinion, for the sort of work done by trading system developers this point is irrelevant and can be ignored. But it is relevant in some other fields, and it certainly is important to purists.

The way I worded this motivational example, we count how many randomized performance scores were at least as great as our job applicant's score and use this to compute a probability that she could have done as well as she did if her method for choosing positions were actually worthless. If this probability is small we assert that her method is probably intelligent. In other words, we just saw an event that would be very unlikely if her method were worthless, so we conclude that her method is probably good.

Statistical purists know that we just did the experiment backwards. To be strictly correct we should set a satisfactorily small *p-value* in advance of doing the experiment and then solve $p=(k+1)/(m+1)$ for k. Only *after* doing this do we perform the experiment, and we base our hiring decision on the number of randomized scores that equal or exceed the job applicant's score. If this count exceeds the count obtained by solving that equation we do not hire the applicant. We hire her only if the count is less than or equal to the k obtained from solving that equation.

Equivalently, and perhaps simpler, is that we hire her only if $(k+1)/(m+1)$ is less than or equal to the probability that *we set in advance*. The key issue that concerns these purists is that instead of computing a p-value first and then deciding if we like it *after we see it*, we set a threshold *in advance* and base our hiring decision on whether the obtained probability is less than or equal to that threshold.

Okay, I admit that there are fields of study in which this order issue is important, but honestly, I have never paid any attention to it in my work designing and testing trading systems. Slap my wrist if you wish. This is my story, and I'm sticking to it.

The Impact of Serial Correlation

There is one critical issue to be aware of when performing a permutation test. In practice this is only rarely a significant limitation in our testing procedures, but it is vitally important that we not violate one simple rule: *we must not permute a series that has significant serial correlation.* The reason is that usually the distribution of our computed performance criterion is impacted by serial correlation. Obviously, when we permute a serially correlated series we destroy that correlation. A criterion computed from a permuted series will not be comparable to this same criterion computed from the original, unpermuted series. So comparing a permuted criterion to the original criterion makes no sense if the original series has serial correlation and the permuted series does not.

Some of the techniques described later in this book involve permuting just one series, and in general this series will have negligible serial correlation. The potential problem that we have to think about generally arises when we are doing paired-series tests like the position/return pairing in the example being considered in this section. I stated earlier that we could permute either the job applicant's chosen positions, or we could permute the market returns. But the positions very likely will have immense serial correlation due to their almost certainly being based on recent market history. For example, our job applicant may consider recent trend in making her position decision. That won't change much day to day. So if we are not allowed to permute a serially correlated series, why do I say we can permute her positions? The answer is that any permutation of the position series is equivalent to a permutation of the return series, and daily market returns have negligible serial correlation. So we can think of it as permuting the daily returns, which is legal.

The problem arises if the return series also has serial correlation. For example, suppose that every day she makes a position choice that will, by design, be in effect for the next three days. The three-day return on adjacent days will have two days in common and hence have great serial correlation. So for paired-series permutation tests, the rule is that *the test is illegal if **both** series have serial correlation.* And know that ***violation of this rule is an extremely serious offense that completely invalidates results.*** It causes the serious error of producing a deceptively small p-value.

Overview of the Bootstrap

Entire books are written on the bootstrap. In my opinion, the very best is "An Introduction to the Bootstrap" by Brad Efron and Robert Tibshirani. You may wish to study that book for more detail. In this short section I'll provide a rough intuitive overview of the technique, and later in this book I'll delve into whatever details are needed for the particular application in that section. I'll provide the intuition, equations, and source code, but if you want the theory behind these things you'll need to get the book just cited or some other reference.

Let's return again to the job applicant example we've been discussing. A job applicant has submitted a series of long/short/neutral positions to be held over the next day. You matched them to next-day market returns; her return for a day is the market return if she had a long position, the negative of the market return if short, and zero if she was out of the market that day. You found that she had a notable net gain. We will be examining her series of daily returns, one value for each day in which she is in the market. (We usually would not want to include in the return series those days in which she is not in the market, because this is just a bunch of zeros. Our real interest is in only those days in which money is on the line.) Thus, her final net gain is the sum of her daily returns.

When we discussed the Monte-Carlo Permutation test on Page 10, we saw that our null hypothesis was that the *pairing* of her positions with next-day market returns was not intelligent, and we hoped to reject that null hypothesis in favor of the alternative that her pairing was intelligent. In our discussion of the bootstrap here, our null hypothesis will be different. It is that the *expected value* of the daily values in her return series is zero (or less), and we hope to reject that in favor of the alternative that the expected value of her daily returns is positive. These are fundamentally different null hypotheses, and it is important to distinguish them.

By the way, this test is easily modified if we want to replace zero in the null hypothesis with a positive value to compensate for trend. This should be clear in the discussions that follow.

At this point we have a series of numbers, her daily returns. We don't care about her long/short/neutral positions; that was needed only for the MCPT which considers pairing. Her net return is the sum of this series of numbers, and it's large enough to get our attention. But is it large enough to convince us that it is due to more than just good luck?

The bootstrap test that we will describe has an advantage over the MCPT in that we do not need position information; just daily (or finer resolution such as intraday bars) returns. Thus it can be used to analyze any trading system for which all we have is periodic returns. On the other hand, it tends to be somewhat less accurate than the MCPT when it computes probabilities involving daily returns. Moreover, if we are testing null hypotheses involving performance measures other than mean daily returns, such as Sharpe ratio and profit factor, the bootstrap becomes distressingly inaccurate, while the MCPT retains high accuracy. So the two tests complement each other nicely.

Enough rambling. Let's move forward. If we were comfortable assuming that the returns followed a normal distribution, or at least that there were no outliers, we could perform a simple one-sample t-test. To do this, we would first compute the standard deviation of the returns, a measure of how much the returns are spread out, and then use a simple formula to estimate how much the mean daily returns of other *hypothetical* samples from the same trading system would be spread out. In other words, the t-test here would consider what would happen if we ran our job applicant's trading system on other time periods and/or markets for which it behaves identically. Because market returns are mostly random, each of these hypothetical runs would have a different mean daily return. Once we know the natural spread of these mean daily returns, we can evaluate the significance of the mean daily return of our applicant.

For example, suppose that based on the spread of the returns in our applicant's system, we compute (using normal distribution assumptions) that 95 percent of the time the mean daily return of a hypothetical run of this same trading system on different market history will be at most 3.7 greater than the true expected daily return. And since our null hypothesis is that the true expected daily return of the trading system is zero, the prior statement is equivalent to saying that, under the assumption that the true expected return is zero, 95 percent of the time we would observe a mean daily return of at most 3.7. This is natural random variation. Only 5 percent of the time will natural random variation cause the mean daily return of a hypothetical run to exceed 3.7.

Now suppose our job applicant had a mean daily return of 2.1. Maybe our original thought was that 2.1 was quite good. But now that we see it in the context of natural random variation it doesn't look so good anymore. On the other hand, suppose her mean daily return was 4.2. That's well outside the natural random spread, so we would be fairly safe in concluding that she was not just lucky; she really has a good trading system.

To be clear, let's review what we just did with a t-test. We estimated the distribution of mean daily returns of that trading system that we could expect by natural random variation and then we compared the achieved results to the spread of natural variation. We estimated that distribution by doing three things:

> 1) We estimated its spread by using the standard deviation of our applicant's daily returns and then applying a simple formula that we won't get into here. See any elementary statistics text if interested.

> 2) We estimated its shape by assuming a normal bell curve

> 3) We assumed that the mean of this distribution is zero, our null hypothesis.

Then we evaluated our job applicant's mean daily return in the context of this distribution of mean daily returns that occurs randomly.

Unfortunately, when we are analyzing returns from trading financial markets, we can almost never assume that the distribution of returns is normal. Outliers (unusually large wins or losses) happen regularly, and even one outlier in the return series completely destroys the validity of the t-test.

Fortunately, the bootstrap lets us do almost the same thing as the t-test, but without having to assume a normal or any other distribution. It does this by assuming that *the spread and shape of the distribution of the returns in our sample series is very close to that of the true population distribution of returns, and that any errors in this assumption will have negligible impact on our computed performance criterion.* Astute readers will question this assumption, and would be right to do so. Indeed, this assumption can sometimes be a bit of a stretch, which explains why bootstrap tests are generally less accurate than permutation tests, which under reasonable conditions are highly accurate. In fact, for some performance measures, such as the Sharpe ratio, this assumption is extremely tenuous. However, for the mean return this assumption is usually valid enough to provide reasonable results.

The basic bootstrap algorithm is simple; we do the same three things we did with the t-test, just slightly differently:

1) We estimate the spread of mean daily returns by computing the spread that we would achieve if her daily returns were a perfect representation of the true population of possible daily returns.

2) We estimate its shape the same way as in Step 1.

3) We assume that the mean of this distribution is zero, our null hypothesis. This is easily done by just shifting her daily returns to have a mean of zero (or whatever value we want to use).

Let's look at this algorithm from a different direction. Because our null hypothesis in this example is that the expected daily return is zero, we center our sample, her daily returns, to have a mean of zero. To do this we just subtract the sample's mean from each daily return. Thus, we are now assuming under the null hypothesis that our sample represents the true population distribution of daily returns from her system if it has an expected return of zero. We repeatedly take a sample (with replacement) from her trading system's centered returns, and compute the mean return of each of these bootstrap samples. After taking many such samples (certainly at least 100, and 1000 or more is not unreasonable) we have a good idea of the natural spread and shape of mean daily returns. We consider where our job applicant's mean daily return lies in this spread range and judge it accordingly.

As a tiny example, suppose our job applicant has the following daily returns: 9, 12, –5, 8, –9, –14, 5, 2. Her net return is the sum of these, 8, giving a mean daily return of 8/8=1. Subtract this mean from every daily return to center the distribution, giving us a revised sample of 8, 11, –6, 7, –10, –15, 4, 1. This is now our representative of the true population distribution of daily returns, though revised to have a mean of zero in accord with our null hypothesis. The important thing to remember is that *we now have an example of how her system's daily returns are spread out by natural random variation*, and we treat this example as if it is a perfect representation of the true distribution of daily returns, though revised to have a mean of zero.

We take a random sample from her centered daily returns, perhaps: 11, 11, –10, –15, 7, 1, 11, –6. The mean of this bootstrap sample is 1.25. Then we take another bootstrap sample and perhaps find that its mean is –0.2. We do another and its mean is 1.4, and so forth. After doing this hundreds or thousands of times we have a good idea of the distribution of mean daily returns that we could expect if we are getting individual daily returns from a population having an expected value of zero (our null hypothesis) but with the same *spread and shape* of returns as our sample. In other words, we now know the natural random spread of mean daily returns we would get if our job applicant's trading system were truly worthless.

The last step is to see where our job applicant's mean daily return (1.0 for the numbers above) lies with respect to the natural random variation one would expect from a worthless system. The relative position of our applicant's mean return tells us how likely it is that she could have been just lucky to get her achieved return. If she beat most or all of the bootstrap mean returns then she stands out from random variation; it's unlikely that she could have done as well as she did by pure luck. Conversely, if a significant fraction of the bootstrapped mean returns exceeded her return, luck could have easily accounted for her return.

There is an even better way to conduct this test, and we will present that algorithm and code on Page 105. However, the explanation just given is the idea behind the technique, and in fact is a reasonable method itself. On a final note, *the warning about serial correlation discussed on Page 14 in the context of the MCPT applies just as much to the bootstrap.* Beware!

Applications in Trading System Development

Before upcoming chapters dig into details regarding applications of Monte-Carlo permutation tests and bootstrap tests in trading system development, it's useful to get a head start by briefly presenting an overview of some topics that will be covered. These are *some* of the situations in which these tests are immensely useful:

- We have already developed and tested a trading system. We just evaluated it on an out-of-sample (*OOS*) dataset and it performed well enough that we are inclined to trade it with real money. But what are the chances that the impressive OOS results we just found could have been due to good luck? The truth is that in order to confidently put a trading system into practice, it must satisfy *two* qualifications:

  1) Its measured OOS performance must be good. Everybody knows about and tests this quality.
  2) There must be small probability that this performance could have been due to good luck. Shockingly few developers take the vital extra step of computing this probability. It doesn't matter how wonderful its OOS performance is if there is a significant probability that this impressive performance could have arisen from good luck. Believe it!

- We are in the earliest stages of developing a trading system. We have a generally defined system but it has one or more optimizable parameters that must be tweaked. Perhaps we have a sophisticated predictive model with numerous model parameters to optimize, or perhaps we have a simple algorithmic system such as a moving-average-crossover system with optimizable lookbacks. The problem is that if we have too many or too strong parameters we may *overfit* the data; our system may learn random noise as if it is an authentic pattern. We can usually detect this by OOS testing, but that is a waste of time and valuable OOS data. *Once we use OOS data, it is no longer truly OOS and, to be strictly correct, can never again be considered OOS.* Thus, it is a treasure to preserve. Luckily, the MCPT provides an excellent way to evaluate the susceptibility of our system to overfitting at the earliest stage of development.

- We have developed what may be called a *model factory*. This is typically a computer program that may try different models, perhaps with different hyper-parameters, perhaps specializing in different market conditions (high/low volatility, up/down trend, etc), perhaps trading different markets or market sectors, and so forth. In other words, this is a machine that throws spaghetti against the wall, watching for something to stick. Invariably, a key part of deciding if a candidate trading system is worth further evaluation is walkforward testing. We already saw that good OOS performance is a necessary but not sufficient condition for having confidence in a trading system. We also need very low probability of the performance having been possibly the product of good luck. The same caveat applies to walkforward testing. The MCPT for walkforward testing is considerably more complex than that for testing a single OOS dataset, but just as necessary. A model factory that does not have walkforward permutation testing built in is a poor and unreliable factory.

- We have a large set of indicators that may or may not have predictive power. For each individual indicator we don't know if its predictive power is restricted to just unusually large values, or unusually small values, or both. We don't even know if that indicator is best used for long systems, or short systems, or both. We just have a lot of indicators and a lot of hope. If we were to try every combination of predictive region and long/short ability for every indicator in our list, we would almost certainly find some amazing 'predictive power' in our trials, even if all indicators are completely worthless. This is because some of our trials are bound to be lucky even though worthless; the chance of winning a major lottery is tiny, but someone still wins despite not having any skill at picking good lottery numbers. An MCPT solves this problem by computing the probability that the clear 'winners' in our ranked performance list could have achieved their exalted position by sheer good luck. This makes it easy to identify potentially powerful indicators while rejecting junk.

- We have multiple competing trading systems. These might be different algorithms operating on the same market, or a single supposedly universal algorithm operating on a variety of markets, or both (multiple systems on multiple markets). There are two questions that should be answered:

  1) Are the best systems, which probably have good apparent performance, really that good or just the luckiest systems?

  2) Is the single best system truly superior to its competitors? More generally, is the rank ordering of the competitors by performance well defined or is quite possibly random?

  It must be made clear that despite superficial similarities, these are completely different questions. The first regards true predictive power versus temporary good luck that will not continue. This is the more important question. In fact, the second question doesn't even matter unless the answer to the first question indicates true power, not just good luck. The second question concerns the best system's ranking relative to the other systems. Is it truly superior to its competitors? Suppose several of our employees present us with different trading systems. Should we focus exclusively on the best performer, or is there evidence that its performance superiority is far from certain? Or suppose we apply our 'universal' trading system to several markets. Should we focus on whichever market has the best performance, or is its superiority uncertain? More generally, how much importance should we give to the quality ranking? An MCPT answers question 1 above, and an interesting randomization test answers question 2.

- Suppose we have a significant block of truly OOS daily (or finer resolution) returns, perhaps from single-use withheld data, perhaps pooled OOS returns from a walkforward, or even from realtime trading results. For example, we may have a year of returns. We can use bootstraps to compute probability-based estimates of performance in the future, assuming that market behavior does not change (a haughty assumption!). We can say, for example, that there is a 90 percent chance that the system's mean annualized daily return is at least some computed value. Using a very complex algorithm we can even compute approximate probabilities for catastrophic drawdowns, an extremely useful thing to know.

2

Core Algorithms

This chapter covers the core algorithms that will be used repeatedly throughout the remainder of this book. These include the standard permutation algorithm (fast and mathematically correct) as well as extensions for single-price and bar data, which require special treatment. The BC_a bootstrap algorithm, which is generally accepted as the most accurate, is presented, although without mathematical justification (which is extremely complex). Finally, I provide in the accompanying code a random number generator that is very good, and more than sufficient for driving the random processes inherent in permutation and bootstrapping.

Basic Permutation

The standard algorithm for permuting a series is fast, mathematically correct (every possible permutation is equally likely), and simple. Stated as a general algorithm, it is as follows:

For k=last element to second element (working backwards through array)
    Randomly choose an element from the first to k, inclusive, with equal probability
    Swap this randomly chosen element with element k

It's that simple. Note that we must include element k among the choices, with the same probability as the other choices. If it is chosen, we will be 'swapping' an element with itself, meaning that no actual swap takes place. Here is that algorithm in C++:

```
i = n_cases ;            // Number remaining to be shuffled
while (i > 1) {          // While at least 2 left to shuffle
  j = (int) (unifrand () * i) ;  // Randomly select a case for swapping
  if (j >= i)            // Should never happen, but be safe
    j = i - 1 ;
  temp = array[--i] ;    // Count down and do the swap
  array[i] = array[j] ;
  array[j] = temp ;
}
```

Most uniform random number generators guaranty that 1.0 will never be returned. But that could be such a disaster in this algorithm that we explicitly make sure it cannot cause a problem.

Some permutation tests involve pairing; an example was seen in the prior chapter when a job candidate provided long/short/neutral market positions that would be paired with daily returns. Although her position decisions almost certainly have serial correlation, daily market returns have only negligibly tiny serial correlation so complete permutation is appropriate.

But occasionally we are in a pairing situation in which both vectors have significant serial correlation (a dangerous situation indeed!). For example, we may have a holding period of several days, in which case daily values of these multiple-day returns will have significant serial correlation due to shared daily returns. Suppose that each day we compute the total return over the next three days. Then adjacent observations will have two days in common, resulting in massive serial correlation.

In this case, complete shuffling is illegal, but a useful alternative is to rotate the elements of the array. Rotation destroys the alignment of the pairs of quantities being related, and hence is likely to produce a distribution of test statistics that is close to the null hypothesis distribution. At the same time, serial correlation is preserved except at the ends where we wrap around. This will almost always tremendously improve the computation of MCPT p-values compared to complete shuffling, which would almost always totally destroy the validity of any computed p-value. But please understand that this is a last-ditch effort, an improvement but not a cure.

Here is the C++ code for rotation. Note that we need a work array for scratch use. Also note that even though it may seem counter-intuitive, for statistical correctness we need to include the possibility that j=0, implying that no rotation is done.

```
j = (int) (unifrand_fast () * n_cases) ;      // Randomly choose the wraparound point
if (j >= n_cases)                             // Should never happen but be safe
   j = n_cases - 1 ;
for (i=0 ; i<n_cases ; i++)                   // Do the rotation into a work array
   work[i] = array[(i+j)%n_cases] ;
for (i=0 ; i<n_cases ; i++)                   // Copy the work array to our rotated array
   array[i] = work[i]  ;
```

Permuting a Single Price Series

The simplest type of price permutation is when we have a series of single prices. The classic example is the closing price of a market each day. It should be obvious that we cannot just permute raw prices. If we did this to the S&P 100 index over several decades we might end up with a price of 10 next to a price of 200. It's a little less obvious but still important that we cannot just permute raw price differences. This is because the average price difference today is several orders of magnitude greater than the average price difference decades ago.

The answer is that we permute differences of logs of prices. Other than normal variation in volatility (which can be large but does not generally have a deterministic trend), the changes in log price tend to be commensurate across time. This provides an effective price permutation algorithm. First we take the log of the market prices, then we compute the series of differences in adjacent log prices. Permute this series of changes and then reconstruct a permuted price series by cumulating these permuted differences, beginning with the original first price. Exponentiate this series to undo taking of logs and get back to the original price domain.

This algorithm has an important property. By definition, the algorithm starts with the original first price for all permutations. When the permuted series is constructed, we add exactly the same set of differences for all permutations, just in a different order. Thus, all permutations end up at the same price, though with any predictable patterns in the interior destroyed. So *any global trend in the price series is exactly replicated in all permutations*. We always start and end at the same prices; we only take different routes getting there. This is important, even critical, in nearly all permutation tests. The most common reason is that trading algorithm returns are usually sensitive to long-term trends. This is especially true if the trading system spends very different amounts of time in long and short positions. Thus, in order for tests performed on permuted price series to be comparable, the long-term trend in every permutation must be the same and identical to that of the original price data.

We now present a C++ class for permuting a single price series. This class assumes that logs of prices have already been taken, and the permuted series is returned still in the log domain, thus requiring exponentiation to return to the original price domain. We invoke the constructor, providing the price series and all parameters, and then we can call the permutation member routine as many times as we wish. The supplied series are returned permuted, so if you need to preserve their original values you will need to do so prior to permuting.

This permutation code allows more than one market to be permuted simultaneously. When multiple markets play a role in a trading system, it is crucial that the permutation swaps be the same in all markets, because this preserves intermarket correlations. Multiple-market trading systems generally rely on this intermarket correlation for making trade decisions and for scoring wins and losses. Thus, in order for tests performed on permuted price histories to be comparable to results obtained from the original price histories, intermarket correlations must be preserved. We want to destroy predictable patterns, which permutation does, without introducing any prejudicial side effects.

Here is the class declaration, followed by the constructor. This code is in PRICE_PERMUTE.CPP. In order to make it easy to access price histories for multiple markets, **prices** is not a vector structured as a matrix. Rather, each element of **prices** is a pointer to an array of prices in chronological order. Thus, **prices[imarket]** is a pointer to the price history of market **imarket**. The work area **changes** is structured the same way.

```
class PricePermute {

public:

   PricePermute (
      int np ,              // Number of prices
      int nmkt ,            // Number of markets
      int index ,           // Index of basis price, one prior to first permuted price
      double **prices       // Input of nmkt by nc price matrix; Output permuted
      ) ;

   ~PricePermute () ;
   void do_permute () ;
```

```
private:
  int ok ;                      // Was memory allocation successful?
  int n_prices ;                // Number of prices
  int n_markets ;               // Number of markets
  int permute_index ;           // Index of first permuted price
  double *basis_prices ;        // Work area for saving basis prices
  double **prices_ptr ;         // Saves pointer to user's price input/output
  double **changes ;            // Work area preserves changes
} ;

PricePermute::PricePermute (
    int np ,                // Number of prices
    int nmkt ,              // Number of markets
    int index ,             // Index of basis price, one prior to first permuted price
    double **prices         // Input of nmkt by nc price matrix; Output permuted
    )
{
  int i, iprice, imarket ;

  n_prices = np ;           // Copy parameters to private areas
  n_markets = nmkt ;
  prices_ptr = prices ;
  permute_index = index + 1 ; // Point to first permuted price
  ok = 1 ;          // Start out optimistic

/*
  Allocate memory
*/

  basis_prices = (double *) malloc ( nmkt * sizeof(double) ) ;
  changes = (double **) malloc ( nmkt * sizeof(double *) ) ;
  if (basis_prices == NULL  ||  changes == NULL) {
    if (basis_prices != NULL) {
      free ( basis_prices ) ;
      basis_prices = NULL ;
      }
    if (changes != NULL) {
      free ( changes ) ;
      changes = NULL ;
      }
    ok = 0 ;
    return ;
    }
```

```
for (imarket=0 ; imarket<n_markets ; imarket++) {
  changes[imarket] = (double *) malloc ( n_prices * sizeof(double) ) ;
  if (changes[imarket] == NULL) {
    for (i=0 ; i<imarket ; i++)
      free ( changes[i] ) ;
    free ( changes ) ;
    free ( basis_prices ) ;
    ok = 0 ;
    return ;
    }
  }

/*
  Compute and save the changes.
  Also save the basis price in case user modifies (ie exponentiates) the permuted prices
*/

for (imarket=0 ; imarket<nmkt ; imarket++) {
  basis_prices[imarket] = prices[imarket][index] ;
  for (iprice=permute_index ; iprice<n_prices ; iprice++)
    changes[imarket][iprice] = prices[imarket][iprice] - prices[imarket][iprice-1] ;
  }
}
```

The **index** parameter is the index of what might be called the 'basis' price. The price at this index will not change; changes will begin at the next price. There are a total of **nc** prices including the basis price. As discussed earlier, the last price also will not change. Only prices after the first (the basis price) and prior to the last will change.

After allocating memory (with a lot of clutter for clean failure) the preparatory code begins by incrementing **index** and saving it in the private member variable **permute_index** that now points to the first permuted price. Then, separately for each market, it finds the difference between each price and the prior price. Recall that we have already taken logs of prices prior to calling this routine. Note that we (perhaps unnecessarily) save the basis price of each market in **basis_prices**. The user may change the returned permuted prices, typically by exponentiating them. We must not begin a permutation from a changed basis price! It must be the original basis price. So, in the spirit of taking no chances, we save the basis prices and recover them later during reconstruction.

The permutation member function shuffles the changes and then reconstructs a permuted price series for each market.

```
void PricePermute::do_permute ()
{
   int i, j, iprice, imarket ;
   double dtemp ;

   // Shuffle the changes, permuting each market the same to preserve correlations
   // We do not include the first case in the shuffling, as it is undefined.

   i = n_prices - permute_index ; // Number remaining to be shuffled
   while (i > 1) {  // While at least 2 left to shuffle
     j = (int) (unifrand() * i) ;
     if (j >= i)   // Should never happen, but be safe
       j = i - 1 ;
     --i ;
     for (imarket=0 ; imarket<n_markets ; imarket++) {
       dtemp = changes[imarket][i+permute_index] ;
       changes[imarket][i+permute_index] = changes[imarket][j+permute_index] ;
       changes[imarket][j+permute_index] = dtemp ;
       }
     } // Shuffle the changes

   // Now rebuild the prices, using the shuffled changes

   for (imarket=0 ; imarket<n_markets ; imarket++) {
     prices_ptr[imarket][permute_index-1] = basis_prices[imarket] ; // Recover basis price
     for (iprice=permute_index ; iprice<n_prices ; iprice++)
       prices_ptr[imarket][iprice] = prices_ptr[imarket][iprice-1] + changes[imarket][iprice] ;
     }
}
```

We use the standard permutation algorithm discussed on Page 24 to shuffle the changes, noting that we offset the shuffled area by **permute_index**, which points one past the basis price. Then we reconstruct the shuffled price array by beginning with the basis price and cumulating the shuffled changes.

If, as usual, we took logs of prices before calling these routines, then we need to exponentiate the returned prices to undo the taking of logs.

Permuting Bars

Permuting bars is significantly more difficult than permuting a single price series. A key tenet of permutation tests is that the statistical properties of the permuted series must be the same as the statistical properties of the original series. Otherwise, trading results obtained from a permuted series, whose predictable patterns have been destroyed, are not comparable to trading results from the unpermuted series. In other words, we must not introduce confounding factors into the test. Permutation must destroy predictable patterns without destroying anything else that impacts test results. We want our permutation test to evaluate performance with versus without predictability, but with all other factors held constant. That can be harder than it might seem. And this is not even a well defined requirement. Consider:

- Despite our best efforts, permutation might damage some statistical property that is crucial to the trading system test but that we didn't even think of.

- We may go to great lengths to preserve some statistical property that is of no importance to the test.

Despite these somewhat discouraging thoughts, in my experience if we take just a few precautions we are covered for virtually every possible trading system test. In particular, we must preserve the distribution of intra-bar price relationships, and we must similarly preserve the distribution of inter-bar price relationships.

Intra-bar price relationships include the net move from open to close, the range between the high and the low, the maximum amount by which the price moves above the open, and the maximum amount by which the price moves below the open. In order to preserve the statistical distribution of these quantities, we can define any given bar by three quantities: The high minus the open, the low minus the open, and the close minus the open. Suppose we pass through the market history and compute these three quantities for each bar. Note that these are not absolute numbers; they are all relative to the open of the bar, whatever that may be. If we permute these triplets, these intra-bar distributions will remain unchanged.

The inter-bar relationships require some thought, because we can easily introduce unnatural price artifacts if we are not careful. Suppose we defined the inter-bar relationship as the change from one open to the next open. Consider a permutation in which a strong down bar (the close is much lower than the open) is followed by a bar with a high positive open-to-open. Then the close of the first bar would be very much lower than the open of the second bar, a situation that would almost never happen in real life.

In fact, bars nearly always open near the close of the prior bar, especially if they are intraday bars. This leads us to the quantity that we permute to vary inter-bar relationships. For each pair of bars we compute the change from the close of one bar to the open of the next bar. We then permute this array of inter-bar changes.

Just as we did for single prices, we want the open of the first bar to be equal for all permutations, and we also want the close of the last bar to be equal. This preserves any global trend, a feature that is crucial for many or most trading system tests. In fact, as we will see later when specific applications are discussed, it is good if the first bar in all permutations is identical to that of the original data.

This leads us to a simple method for reconstructing a bar series after the intra-bar and inter-bar relationships have been permuted. Begin with the first bar of the original data. Add to its close the first permuted value of the inter-bar series, the close-to-next-open differences. This gives us the open of the next bar. Then use the next permuted intra-bar triplet to give us the high, low, and close of this bar. The close of this bar plus the next permuted inter-bar difference provides the open of the following bar, and so forth.

This method of permuting bars preserves the distribution of all intra-bar and inter-bar relationships, also preserves the global trend, but completely destroys any predictable patterns in the market history. This algorithm should be usable for nearly any trading system test. However, do note the warning about redistribution of day range extremes discussed on Page 39. This small flaw may impact some trading systems.

Here is the class declaration for the **BarPermute** class. We will invoke the constructor, specifying the four price arrays that will serve as both input of the original bars and output of the permuted bars. As we did for price permutation, these four quantities are arrays of pointers. For example, open[imarket] is a pointer to the chronological open prices for the specified market. Also as we did for price permutation, index is the index in the price history of the basis bar, the bar that does not change under permutation and from which the permuted series is reconstructed.

```
class BarPermute {

public:
  BarPermute (
     int np ,                  // Number of prices
     int nmkt ,                // Number of markets
     int index ,               // Index of basis bar, one prior to first permuted price
     double **open ,           // Input of nmkt by nc opens
     double **high ,           // Input of nmkt by nc highs
     double **low ,            // Input of nmkt by nc lows
     double **close            // Input of nmkt by nc closes
     ) ;
  ~BarPermute () ;
  void do_permute () ;

private:
  int ok ;                     // Was memory allocation successful?
  int n_prices ;               // Number of prices (bars)
  int n_markets ;              // Number of markets
  int permute_index ;          // Index of first permuted price
  double *basis_open ;         // Work area for saving basis prices (bars)
  double *basis_high ;         // Ditto
  double *basis_low ;          // Ditto
  double *basis_close ;        // Ditto
  double **open_ptr ;          // Saves pointer to user's price input/output
  double **high_ptr ;          // Ditto
  double **low_ptr ;           // Ditto
  double **close_ptr ;         // Ditto
  double **rel_open ;          // Work area of n_markets arrays np long
  double **rel_high ;          // Ditto
  double **rel_low ;           // Ditto
  double **rel_close ;         // Ditto
} ;
```

The constructor copies the parameters to private areas. When it saves the index it adds one so that permute_index points to the first unpermuted bar.

```
BarPermute::BarPermute (
      int np ,                  // Number of prices
      int nmkt ,                // Number of markets
      int index ,               // Index of basis price, one prior to first permuted price
      double **open ,           // Input of nmkt by nc opens
      double **high ,           // Input of nmkt by nc highs
      double **low ,            // Input of nmkt by nc lows
      double **close            // Input of nmkt by nc closes
      )
{
   int i, iprice, imarket ;

   n_prices = np ;              // Copy parameters to private areas
   n_markets = nmkt ;
   open_ptr = open ;
   high_ptr = high ;
   low_ptr = low ;
   close_ptr = close ;
   permute_index = index + 1 ; // Point to first permuted price
```

The memory allocation code in PRICE_PERMUTE.CPP includes clean failure in case of insufficient memory. That is omitted here for clarity.

```
   basis_open = (double *) malloc ( 4 * n_markets * sizeof(double) ) ;
   rel_open = (double **) malloc ( 4 * n_markets * sizeof(double *) ) ;

   basis_high = basis_open + n_markets ;     // We do just one allocation above, 4 times
   basis_low = basis_high + n_markets ;      // larger than needed, then split it here
   basis_close = basis_low + n_markets ;
   rel_high = rel_open + n_markets ;         // Do the same for the change arrays
   rel_low = rel_high + n_markets ;
   rel_close = rel_low + n_markets ;

   for (imarket=0 ; imarket<n_markets ; imarket++) { // Allocate changes for each market
     rel_open[imarket] = (double *) malloc ( 4 * n_prices * sizeof(double) ) ;
     rel_high[imarket] = rel_open[imarket] + n_prices ;
     rel_low[imarket] = rel_high[imarket] + n_prices ;
     rel_close[imarket] = rel_low[imarket] + n_prices ;
     }
```

For each market, do the following:

1) Save the basis bar. This is necessary because the caller has almost certainly taken logs of prices before invoking the constructor, and therefore may exponentiate the permuted series. Since the same arrays serve as both input and output, exponentiation would destroy the basis bar.

2) Compute **rel_open** as the difference between each bar's open and the prior bar's close. This is the *inter-bar* data discussed earlier.

3) Compute **rel_high**, **rel_low**, and **rel_close** as the trio that defines the *intra-bar* behavior discussed earlier.

```
for (imarket=0 ; imarket<n_markets ; imarket++) {
   basis_open[imarket] = open[imarket][index] ;
   basis_high[imarket] = high[imarket][index] ;
   basis_low[imarket] = low[imarket][index] ;
   basis_close[imarket] = close[imarket][index] ;
   for (iprice=permute_index ; iprice<n_prices ; iprice++) {
      rel_open[imarket][iprice] = open[imarket][iprice] - close[imarket][iprice-1] ;
      rel_high[imarket][iprice] = high[imarket][iprice] - open[imarket][iprice] ;
      rel_low[imarket][iprice] = low[imarket][iprice] - open[imarket][iprice] ;
      rel_close[imarket][iprice] = close[imarket][iprice] - open[imarket][iprice] ;
      }
   }
}
```

We call **do_permute()** to return a permuted bar array. We must separately shuffle the inter-bar gaps and the intra-bar trios. In both cases we will be shuffling **n_prices - permute_index** terms. This code first shuffles the trios and then the gaps. The standard shuffling algorithm shown on Page 24 is used both times.

```
void BarPermute::do_permute ()
{
   int i, j, iprice, imarket ;
   double dtemp ;

   i = n_prices - permute_index ; // Number remaining to be shuffled
```

```
while (i > 1) {  // While at least 2 left to shuffle
  j = (int) (unifrand() * i) ;
  if (j >= i)  // Should never happen, but be safe
    j = i - 1 ;
  --i ;
  for (imarket=0 ; imarket<n_markets ; imarket++) { // Shuffle the intra-bar trios
    dtemp = rel_high[imarket][i+permute_index] ;
    rel_high[imarket][i+permute_index] = rel_high[imarket][j+permute_index] ;
    rel_high[imarket][j+permute_index] = dtemp ;
    dtemp = rel_low[imarket][i+permute_index] ;
    rel_low[imarket][i+permute_index] = rel_low[imarket][j+permute_index] ;
    rel_low[imarket][j+permute_index] = dtemp ;
    dtemp = rel_close[imarket][i+permute_index] ;
    rel_close[imarket][i+permute_index] = rel_close[imarket][j+permute_index] ;
    rel_close[imarket][j+permute_index] = dtemp ;
    }
  } // Shuffle the intra-bar trios

// Separately shuffle the close-to-open changes,
// permuting each market the same to preserve correlations.

i = n_prices - permute_index ; // Number remaining to be shuffled
while (i > 1) {  // While at least 2 left to shuffle
  j = (int) (unifrand() * i) ;
  if (j >= i)  // Should never happen, but be safe
    j = i - 1 ;
  --i ;
  for (imarket=0 ; imarket<n_markets ; imarket++) {
    dtemp = rel_open[imarket][i+permute_index] ;
    rel_open[imarket][i+permute_index] = rel_open[imarket][j+permute_index] ;
    rel_open[imarket][j+permute_index] = dtemp ;
    }
  } // Shuffle the close-to-open changes
```

The last step is to rebuild the permuted series. The basis bar remains unchanged, so we recover it from where it was saved in the constructor call. We begin reconstruction at the bar immediately following the basis bar. The open of each new bar is the close of the prior bar (close_ptr[imarket][iprice-1]) plus the next permuted inter-bar gap (rel_open[imarket][iprice]). The high, low, and close of this new bar are all relative to the open of the bar.

```
for (imarket=0 ; imarket<n_markets ; imarket++) {
  open_ptr[imarket][permute_index-1] = basis_open[imarket] ; // Recover basis price
  high_ptr[imarket][permute_index-1] = basis_high[imarket] ;
  low_ptr[imarket][permute_index-1] = basis_low[imarket] ;
  close_ptr[imarket][permute_index-1] = basis_close[imarket] ;

  for (iprice=permute_index ; iprice<n_prices ; iprice++) {   // Rebuild permuted series
    open_ptr[imarket][iprice] = close_ptr[imarket][iprice-1] + rel_open[imarket][iprice] ;
    high_ptr[imarket][iprice] = open_ptr[imarket][iprice] + rel_high[imarket][iprice] ;
    low_ptr[imarket][iprice] = open_ptr[imarket][iprice] + rel_low[imarket][iprice] ;
    close_ptr[imarket][iprice] = open_ptr[imarket][iprice] + rel_close[imarket][iprice] ;
    } // For iprice
  } // For imarket
} // End of do_permute()
```

Permuting Intraday Data

Intraday data can be represented as shown in Figure 2.1 below. We have a 'basis' day, followed by an overnight gap, then the first permuted day, another overnight gap, another day, and so forth. Each day can be composed of individual prices (ticks) or bars of any size.

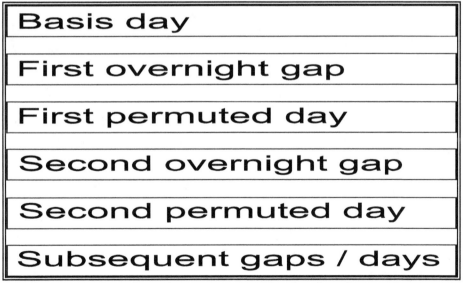

Figure 2.1 Intraday price representation showing days and gaps

I won't provide specific code for permuting intraday data, because the code is highly dependent on how you store the information. However, the process is a simple extension of what we just saw for bar data. We permute the (log) prices or bars within each day, *separately for each day*, exactly as has been discussed in the prior sections. (We do not permute the prices/bars in the basis day.) We also compute the vector of overnight gaps, the difference between the closing price of one day and the opening price of the next day. This gap vector is permuted.

In order to rebuild the permuted dataset, it's easiest if, separately for each day, we subtract the open of each day from all prices in that day, which of course leaves each day opening at a price of zero. Also, rather than trying to permute entire blocks of intraday data, we leave them in their original order and storage format, and instead permute an index vector that defines the order in which permuted days are appended. Then, to rebuild the permuted intraday data, we begin with the basis day, unchanged. Add to its close the first permuted overnight gap. This gives the amount to be added to each price within the next day. Repeat this process until all days have been included. Here is this algorithm stated more concisely. First, initialize:

1) Compute the vector of overnight gaps (close of one day to open of the next day).

2) Separately for each day *except the basis day*, subtract the open of that day from all prices in that day, including the open (thereby leaving the open at zero).

3) Initialize an index vector of integers 0, 1, 2, ... This vector contains as many elements as there are days to be permuted.

Repeat as often as desired to create permutations:

1) Separately for each day *except the basis day*, permute the data for that day using either the single price or the bar algorithm described in prior sections.

2) Permute the vector of overnight gaps.

3) Permute the vector of indices that were initialized in Step 3 above.

4) Let the basis day be the first 'permuted' day.

5) Select the day (already permuted in Step 1 above) identified by the first permuted index. Add to each of its prices the close of the basis day as well as the first permuted overnight gap.

6) Select the day identified by the second permuted index. Add to each of its prices the close of the prior day as well as the second permuted overnight gap.

7) Repeat Step 6 above until all days are appended.

In case you are wondering why each individual day must be permuted separately... Suppose we pooled the intraday changes into one big permutation pool and randomly selected our new daily data from this pool. This would tend toward homogeneity in daily ranges. As we built each day we would get some big jumps and some little jumps, and we would end up with each day having about the same net change. This is not representative of real-life daily action. By internally permuting each day separately we preserve the statistical distribution of daily net changes. And obviously the distribution of overnight gaps remains unchanged as well. Finally, I leave it as a simple exercise for the reader to confirm that the long-term trend of the market also remains unchanged.

This algorithm should perform well for many intraday trading systems. Its one apparent flaw is that changes in intraday volatility will be scattered across the permuted data instead of being clumped as is the usual situation. This may cause a problem for some trading systems. In other words, in real life we will have periods of days, weeks, or even months when day ranges are unusually high or low. However, when we shuffle across the entire historical time period we randomly distribute unusually high or low day ranges, which is unnatural. In my experience this is rarely, if ever a problem, but you should know about it. I am not aware of any practical fix.

What About Night Sessions?

Including overnight sessions is a trivial extension of the algorithm we just saw. In addition to separately permuting each day session (except the basis section), we also individually permute each night session. We also have to compute and permute *two* gaps, the night-close-to-day-open, and the day-close-to-night-open. We also have to initialize and subsequently permute *two* index vectors, one for selecting day sessions and one for selecting night sessions.

To rebuild a permuted price series, begin with the unchanged basis day session. Add to its close the first permuted day-to-night gap to get the open of the night session, which has been individually permuted already. Add to its close the first permuted night-to-day gap in order to get the open of the next day session. Repeat.

3

Permutation Test Applications

This chapter presents some specific applications of permutation tests for trading system development. The core algorithms discussed in the prior chapter will employed throughout. In each case I'll explain the goal of the test, show how it is performed, and provide source code for an example of how it can be implemented. For these demonstrations I'll employ trivially simple (and worthless!) trading systems hard-coded in C++. I'll also use several decades of market history day bars.

Early-Stage Testing for Overfitting

Typically, the first step in the development of a financial trading system is defining the decision-making methodology. This is the algorithm that examines recent market history and decides whether to open or close a position in the market, and it's based on our theory of how markets behave. But this methodology usually includes one or more parameters that must be tweaked to optimize performance. For example, you might conceive a theory that if a short-term moving average crosses above a long-term moving average, the market is entering a period of upward trend, and hence you should take a long position. Conversely, if it crosses below you should be short. But how far should you look back for each of these two moving averages? These two lookbacks are optimizable parameters. We need to tweak them to obtain the best possible performance.

There are primarily two ways in which our decision-making methodology can fail, one obvious and one less so. First, it may be that our idea of how the market operates is rubbish, or our implementation that is supposedly based on this idea is poorly executed. Whatever the case, the net result is that the performance of our trading system is poor, even after optimization. However, poor performance will be quickly apparent and we will likely go back to the drawing board soon. Thus, we will not often perform a permutation test with the goal of confirming that our trading system is effectively capitalizing on market patterns. That would be killing a gnat with a sledge hammer.

The second way our decision-making methodology can fail is much more subtle, and sadly ignored by too many developers. It may seem counter-intuitive, but it's possible (and common!) for our implementation to be *too powerful*. Market moves are driven by two types of forces. One type is predictable patterns. For example, trends tend to continue until they become exhausted or a news item throws a monkey wrench into the market. As another example, very short-term departures from historical behavior tend to quickly correct back to normality in an effect called *mean reversion*. These are the sorts of predictable market patterns that we seek to exploit.

The other force that drives markets is random noise, or at least forces that appear to be random because we cannot explain or predict them. The important point about random noise is that it is not repeatable. The noise that is present in the dataset we use for tweaking our trading system will not continue in the same 'pattern' when we put the system to work.

Because of these two very different and opposing forces, we walk a fine line when we develop a trading system. It must be powerful enough to detect and use legitimate market patterns, those that can be expected to continue into the future. But it must not be so powerful that it fits everything it sees, mistaking random noise for legitimate patterns. If this happens, trade decisions made when the system is put to use will be garbage, because 'patterns' that the system learned during tweaking for optimal performance will not continue. This phenomenon, which is far more dangerous than most developers realize, is called *overfitting*. This is a good term, because an overly powerful decision-making methodology goes beyond fitting legitimate patterns, and also fits random patterns.

There is a high correlation between overfitting and the number of optimizable parameters. If your trading system has just one optimizable parameter, it is not likely to overfit. For example, suppose you have a mean reversion system that looks for a large gap between the most recent price and the prior price. Your only optimizable parameter might be the size of the gap, perhaps expressed as a percentage of the prior price. If the price jump exceeds the optimal threshold, you take a position that will show a profit if the price reverts back toward the prior price. It is relatively unlikely that such a system will mistake noise for authentic patterns, because the 'pattern' of price moves after noise-driven jumps will be random. Only authentic mean reversion in the market will have behavior that is consistent enough for your trading system to capitalize on it. Of course, such a primitive system is also unlikely to make enough money to be worth trading, so in this simple example overfitting is a moot point.

Conversely, suppose you have a sophisticated neural-network-based predictive model that has dozens of optimizable parameters. A good optimizer will be able to tweak such a trading system so effectively that it will learn a wide variety of noise 'patterns', making a ton of money in the training period, and then failing miserably when put to use trading real money.

I hope by now I have convinced you that it is imperative that you investigate the possibility of overfitting before laying real money on the table. Of course, there are indirect but effective ways of doing this without permutation tests. The venerable old standard is to hold out a batch of market history, optimizing the parameters on just a subset of your available market history, and then testing your trained model on the held-out (*out-of-sample* or *OOS*) time period. Chances are that if your trading system is overfitting, its performance on the OOS data will be poor. A more sophisticated version of this process is walkforward testing, in which you train (optimize parameters) on a block of data, test on a block that immediately follows the training set, and then move the training and testing windows forward, repeating this training/testing cycle several times. This testing process is fairly effective at detecting overfitting, although we are always better off catching this problem sooner.

Apart from those weaknesses yet to be discussed, I must point out now that there is an even greater problem with out-of-sample testing, and which is woefully ignored by most developers. It is this: *After you have used out-of-sample data EVEN ONCE it is no longer out-of-sample.* I can't emphasize this strongly enough. Suppose you have a candidate trading system that performs well on your early backtests, so you walk it forward and discover, to your annoyance, that its performance is poor. You have now, in a very real sense, *wasted* your out-of-sample data on testing a trading system that you could (or at least should) have known in advance would be likely to fail.

How can we call this wasting the OOS data? After all, if you go back to the drawing board, develop a new trading system using early data and then walk it forward using the same OOS data that you used when testing the prior system, you are still training and testing on different data. Surely that's legitimate, right?

Wrong. Very, very wrong. The reason is a phenomenon called *selection bias*. I won't take the time right now to explain it in detail. I'll approach this topic from a different direction later, on Page 76. Also, I covered the topic in great depth in my earlier book "Testing and Tuning Market Trading Systems" published by the Apress division of Springer. Here I'll just provide a general explanation. One way of putting it is to say that if you use supposedly out-of-sample data more than once to help you select the best of two or more competing systems, that data inherently becomes part of your training set. You are using that supposedly OOS data for optimization, in the sense that you are selecting the best from among two or more competing systems. So your ultimately selected trading system is susceptible to overfitting, and will have a strong optimistic bias, as a direct consequence of the selection process.

There is a general concept that is one of the most important considerations in trading system development:

Your out-of-sample data is precious! Preserve it for as long as you possibly can, because it will be truly out-of-sample only once, and getting more is expensive if not impossible. Use it only when you have performed so many other tests that you have high confidence in your trading system.

By now you understand the motivation to begin testing as early as possible. Not only do you want to avoid wasting your own valuable time and computer resources in a long series of tests on a system that ultimately fails, but even more importantly you do not want to waste your precious OOS data. Luckily, there is a simple permutation test that can usually tell you quickly, at the earliest stages of trading system development, whether your trading system is susceptible to overfitting. If you find this to be so, you can go back to the drawing board before wasting any more time, money, or precious OOS data.

Now would be a good time to review the basics of Monte-Carlo permutation testing, the section that began on Page 10. That section focused on tests in which we have two series whose observations are paired, and we shuffle one of the series to destroy any actual relationship between the series. Here we will instead shuffle our market(s), thereby destroying any predictive information while usually not destroying any other important properties of the market, such as long-term trend and overall volatility.

The underlying principle is the same, whether we are shuffling to destroy pairing relationships or shuffling to destroy predictable patterns. We run our trading system on the data that we consider to be the training set, and we compute a performance criterion. Then we shuffle the market history m times, recomputing the performance criterion for each. Count the number k of times that the criterion for a shuffled run equals or exceeds that for the original, unshuffled data. Then $p=(k+1)/(m+1)$ is the p-value associated with the test.

This p-value can be interpreted as the approximate probability that, if the trading system were truly worthless, we could have obtained performance at least as good as what we did obtain. Note that the term *worthless* here is not limited to weakness, the inability to learn predictable patterns. This term also includes excessive power, the counterproductive ability to learn random patterns of noise as if they were legitimate market patterns. An effective trading system must lie in the sweet spot between too little and too much power, strong enough to learn tradable patterns but not so strong that it learns noise as well. If a trading system is too powerful, typically due to too many optimizable parameters, it will perform nearly as well on the permuted market histories as the original, with the result that many permuted performances will equal or exceed that of the original, producing a p-value that is not small. I typically demand a p-value less than 0.05 as a minimal standard, and I'm not truly happy with a system unless the p-value is under 0.01.

Here is a brief aside directed mainly at readers with some statistical background, although everyone should read this. If we repeat this permutation test many times, it is likely that sooner or later we will obtain an excellent test result (small p-value) from a truly worthless system. For example, if the trading system is worthless, there is still a 5 percent probability that we will get a p-value of 0.05 or less, and a 1 percent probability that we will even see a wonderful p-value of 0.01 or less. This is a strong argument for performing this test only when it is warranted.

My own practice is to perform it only on trading systems that have already shown outstanding in-sample (training set) performance. Remember that the training process introduces significant, often massive optimistic bias. Thus, I want to see numerous trades (to ensure stability), an outstanding equity curve with minimal drawdown, a large profit factor, and so forth, before I advance to performing a permutation test for overfitting.

There's one last issue to wrap up before concluding with a practical demonstration. What about the performance criterion for comparing the original and permuted results? My preferred criterion is the profit factor based on the log of market prices, with open positions marked to the market at the highest resolution possible. Of course, if you are quoting performance figures to a client, you should base any performance figures on actual prices. But in an optimization or testing procedure you should almost always compute your performance figures using logs of prices. The reason is that you are probably operating over a long period of market history, during which average market prices may vary over a large range. For example, early in your training/testing period prices may be around 50, while a decade later prices may be around 200. Operating on raw prices gives excessive weight to time periods with higher prices, while operating on log prices gives price changes equal weight across time.

Why use profit factor instead of figures like total return or mean return per trade? Or Sharpe ratio? It has been my experience over several decades that of all performance measures, profit factor is the most reliable in that the correlation between its in-sample and out-of-sample values is generally highest of all competitors. This is probably because it inherently includes a measure of risk, rewarding consistency of returns.

And why mark it to market at the highest resolution possible? The simple answer is that having more measurements going into the final figure provides more accurate and stable results. For those interested in more information, my book "Testing and Tuning Market Trading Systems" presents a detailed analysis of the arguments for using high-resolution profit factor in training and testing.

A Practical Example

In order to demonstrate this technique I wrote a small program that runs in a Windows Command Console. Complete source code is in the OVERFIT directory, which includes RAND.CPP for random number generation, PRICE_PERMUTE.CPP for the core permutation routines, and OVERFIT.CPP for the main program.

This demonstration program implements a trivial moving-average-crossover system. The routine **opt_params()** executes this system for a variety of long-term and short-term lookbacks and returns the optimal profit factor, along with the corresponding optimal lookbacks. If you wanted to use the OVERFIT program to test your own trading system, you would replace this routine with your own trading system. Just to be clear on the operation of this routine, I'll list it here and walk through the code, explaining any potentially unclear sections. Please understand that this routine has nothing to do with the main topic of this section, permutation testing for overfitting. This is just the silly little trading system that's being tested.

Here is the calling parameter list and variable declarations. You don't have to use log prices; it's perfectly legal to use raw prices, and you maybe would want to do so if the prices don't have huge variation over the historical period, but in the majority of cases you will want to use log prices for the reasons discussed earlier.

```
double opt_params (   // Returns optimal profit factor
  int nprices ,       // Number of log prices in X
  double *prices ,    // Log prices
  int *short_term ,   // Returns optimal short-term lookback
  int *long_term      // Returns optimal long-term lookback
  )
{
  int i, j, ishort, ilong, ibestshort, ibestlong ;
  double short_sum, long_sum, short_mean, long_mean, best_perf ;
  double ret, win_sum, lose_sum ;
```

I initialize the best-so-far profit factor to a huge negative number and then have nested loops that do a brute-force search of all combinations of long-term and short-term lookbacks. I picked 252 as the upper limit for the long-term lookback, as this is a year of daily trades. I arbitrarily limit the short-term lookback to half of the current trial long-term lookback. Neither of these choices are magical; feel free to change them or make them user parameters. Then, as we are about to test a parameter set, initialize the sum of wins and sum of losses to essentially zero. We don't want to divide by zero later, so I actually initialize these sums to a value so small that the first time a real win or loss is summed in this initial value will vanish.

```
best_perf = -1.e60 ;                              // Best performance across all trials
for (ilong=2 ; ilong<252 ; ilong++) {            // Trial long-term lookback
  for (ishort=1 ; ishort<=ilong/2 ; ishort++) {  // Trial short-term lookback
    win_sum = lose_sum = 1.e-60 ;                // Cumulates for profit factor
```

For the currently tested lookbacks, we execute this trading system across as much of the market history as is possible. The earliest we can start is the price at which we have ilong prices available, and we have to stop one before the end of the history because profits are computed by looking one price ahead of wherever we are in decision making. For the first decision case we explicitly compute the long-term and short-term sums, noting that because these summing periods overlap we can compute the short-term sum first and then pick up where we left off for the long-term sum. From then on we save time by just updating the sums, adding in the new price and subtracting out the oldest.

```
for (i=ilong-1 ; i<nprices-1 ; i++) {   // Compute performance across history
  if (i == ilong-1) { // Find the sums for the first valid case.
    short_sum = 0.0 ;                 // Cumulates short-term lookback sum
    for (j=i ; j>i-ishort ; j--)
      short_sum += prices[j] ;
    long_sum = short_sum ;            // Cumulates long-term lookback sum
    while (j>i-ilong)
      long_sum += prices[j--] ;
    }
  else {                             // Update the moving averages
    short_sum += prices[i] - prices[i-ishort] ;
    long_sum += prices[i] - prices[i-ilong] ;
    }
```

Dividing the sums by the number of prices in them gives the moving average. If the short-term MA is above the long-term MA we take a long position, scoring our return (profit or loss) as the next price minus this price. Conversely, if we have the opposite crossing we take a short position. In the unusual situation that the two are equal we stay out of the market. If we just showed a profit, cumulate it into the winning sum, while if we suffered a loss cumulate it into the sum of losses.

```
short_mean = short_sum / ishort ;
long_mean = long_sum / ilong ;

if (short_mean > long_mean)        // Long position
  ret = prices[i+1] - prices[i] ;
else if (short_mean < long_mean)   // Short position
  ret = prices[i] - prices[i+1] ;
else
  ret = 0.0 ;

if (ret > 0.0)     // A positive return is a win
  win_sum += ret ;
else
  lose_sum -= ret ;

} // For i, summing performance for this trial
```

Finally, keep track of the optimal values and return them when done.

```
if (win_sum / lose_sum > best_perf) {
  best_perf = win_sum / lose_sum ;
  ibestshort = ishort ;
  ibestlong = ilong ;
  }
 } // For ishort, all short-term lookbacks
} // For ilong, all long-term lookbacks

*short_term = ibestshort ;
*long_term = ibestlong ;

return best_perf ;
}
```

Now we get to the interesting part. I'll skip all the mundane code for reading market history; you can find that in OVERFIT.CPP. The user has specified as nreps the number of replications, which includes the original, unpermuted test. Recall that the p-value is $(k+1)/(m+1)$ where m is the number of permutations (not including the original, unpermuted run), and k is the number of permuted values that equal or exceed that of the original. Even though the trading system in this example uses just the closing price series, we permute bars in this example code to make it easier for the reader to just drop in his or her own trading system, which may use bar data. The code for the **BarPermute** class is in PRICE_PERMUTE.CPP.

We loop through all replications. The first one is the original test, without permutation. So if irep=0 we allocate the **BarPermute** object and compute the optimal lookbacks and profit factor. We may wish to report these optimal values to the user here. We also initialize count, the counter k of permuted trials whose criterion equals or exceeds that of the original, to 1 in deference to the numerator of $k+1$. If we are past the first, unpermuted replication, we permute the prices and compute the optimal profit factor. If this equals or exceeds the original, increment the counter. When done, divide to get the p-value. It's that simple.

```
BarPermute *bp_ptr ;

for (irep=0 ; irep<nreps ; irep++) {

   if (irep == 0) {
     bp_ptr = new BarPermute ( nprices , 1 , 0 , &open , &high , &low , &close ) ;
     original = opt_params ( nprices , close , &opt_short , &opt_long ) ;
     // Optionally print optimal lookbacks and profit factor here
     count = 1 ;
     }

   else {
     bp_ptr->do_permute () ;
     opt_return = opt_params ( nprices , close , &opt_short , &opt_long ) ;
     if (opt_return >= original)
        ++count ;
     }

   pval = (double) count / (double) nreps ) ;
```

The OVERFIT program is called with two parameters:

```
OVERFIT  Nreps  MarketFile
```

The *Nreps* parameter specifies how many replications are to be done, including the original, unpermuted run. The *MarketFile* parameter specifies the market history file, each of whose lines specifies the date as YYYYMMDD, the open, high, low, and close. Spaces, tabs, or commas may be used as delimiters. Anything after these prices, such as volume, is ignored. Here are two sample lines from a market history file:

```
19880211 122.32 122.89 121.42 121.92 4015
19880212 121.92 123.37 121.82 122.72 3544
```

I ran this program with two datasets and got results that are not surprising. Using OEX from its inception through the end of 2019 the following results were obtained:

Profit factor based on log prices = 1.092
optimal long lookback = 243 short lookback = 17
p-value for null hypothesis that system is worthless = 0.3700

And using QQQ from its inception through the end of 2019 the following results were obtained:

Profit factor based on log prices = 1.118
optimal long lookback = 251 short lookback = 14
p-value for null hypothesis that system is worthless = 0.0900

In both cases the profit factor is so small that if this were a real-life test I would not go on to run the test for overfitting. I would want to see an optimized profit factor of at least 1.4 or so, and ideally even more. Not surprisingly, neither p-value is small enough to get my attention. In this case I suspect that these insignificant p-values are not due to overfitting as much as they are due to the trading system simply being an incorrect representation of true market patterns. I will say, though, that I find it interesting to see the optimal lookbacks for the two quite different markets to be so close. Maybe it's just coincidence or maybe it's real, though weak.

Testing a Fully Developed System

Many trading system developers grit their teeth and hold out a block of recent market history as a final acid test of their system. This block is strictly withheld from all development, including initial design, tweaking, walkforward tests, permutation tests, and so forth. It takes a lot of willpower to hold back the most current data you have all the way through development, but there is a good reason for doing so. If you wait until you have what you believe is a fully tweaked system, complete and ready to go, and then test it on your withheld data, you will be rewarded with a truly unbiased estimate of future performance. That is priceless.

Unfortunately, most developers look at only the attained performance and rejoice if it is good. That's just half of the battle. What is also needed is an estimate of how likely the 'good' achieved performance could be if the trading system were truly worthless. Suppose you were to learn that there was a 25 percent chance that even a worthless system could have done at least this well on the withheld period. I sure hope you would rethink your enthusiasm. At the end of this section I'll present a short but scary demonstration of this phenomenon.

Figure 3.1 on the next page depicts a tiny example of this holdout process. In this example, we have a total of 10 prices, indexed from 0 through 9. Our development plan decrees that the first 7 prices are used for the entire development process, with the last 3 prices completely ignored. The indicators used by this trading system have a maximum lookback of 2, including the current price. Returns are computed as the price change from the decision price to the next price. As shown in that figure, the first trading decision that can be made during training is at index 1 (which gives us our required lookback of 2), a fact that is not terribly important to this discussion but that will clarify something in the code presented later.

The most important aspect of that figure is the price at index 6. This price, the last price in the training period, plays multiple roles in this discussion. The last price at which a trade decision can be made is the prior price, index 5 here, because the price change from 5 to 6 is the last return that we can consider during training. The first price change that will be used when testing the withheld (OOS) set is that from 6 to 7.

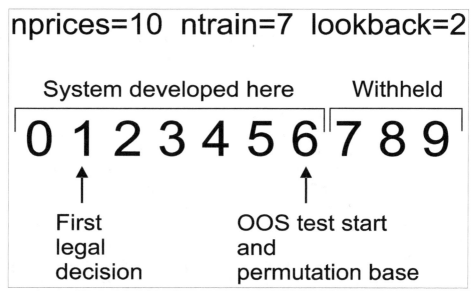

Figure 3.1 Testing a preserved OOS history period

This tells us a fact that may seem counter-intuitive at first. When we come to testing the OOS set, the first trade decision is made on the last price in the training set. Isn't that producing overlap in the training and testing periods? No, because it's price *changes* that define returns, and when we make a trade decision on the last price in the training period we then have a return that is determined by the first price in the OOS period. That change never appeared in the training process, so we have correct separation.

I should note a couple things about this view of developing and testing a trading system. I am assuming that the return is defined as the price change from the time the trade decision is made to the next price. Experienced traders will raise two main objections to this representation. First, they will say that this does not consider trading systems that have extended positions, perhaps holding a day-bar system's position for many days. My response is that we treat each day individually. If we open a position that will be held for several days, then on each subsequent day we treat it as if the system said to hold that position for one more day, and we would take the price change to the next day as another return. When we eventually come to the end of the development period, we just terminate the process. This is not only a perfectly legitimate approach, but it is good (many would argue necessary) because, as I have emphasized before, when computing performance figures like profit factor we always want returns to be quantized at the highest resolution possible.

The other objection is somewhat more reasonable, though certainly not a deal killer. It is difficult, if not impossible, to open a trade at the same price as when the decision was made. For example, if we are trading day bars, when we know the close of the day, the market is by definition closed, so we cannot open a trade at that price. A more conservative approach would be to define the return of the trade decision as the price move from the open of the next day to the open of the following day. On the other hand, that approach severely complicates testing algorithms and, in my opinion, is overkill. For one thing, we can watch prices during the day and define the 'close' as the price as of a short time before the official close, thereby enabling us to get in and out of a trade at a price very close to the decision price. And in my experience, even that's overkill. For developing and testing trading systems, using close-to-close returns is completely acceptable and provides results substantially identical to using more conservative methods. If you were reporting performance to investors you would probably want to use a more conservative measure, but at the development stage close-to-close is nearly always fine.

Besides being the first decision price for the OOS test period, the last price in the training (development) time period is also the permutation base. Recall from prior discussions of price and bar permutation that we need a baseline price or bar from which permutation is built. This baseline is not changed by permutation; only those prices (or bars) beyond it are permuted.

Why not permute the entire time period, including the development period? The answer is crucial, so just to be absolutely clear... ***You must not include the development period in the permutation***. The reason is that the returns that potentially go into computation of the performance criterion for the permuted runs *must* be exactly the same returns that went into computing the performance criterion for the original, unpermuted run. What if the development period had some unusual returns, particularly large perhaps, or perhaps a string of nearly zero returns. If we allow permutation to swap some of these oddballs into the test period, computation of the performance criterion will be impacted in ways not commensurate with computation for the original, unpermuted run. By permuting only those changes that are past the last training price we ensure that order is destroyed but other properties suffer minimal distortion.

Example Code and a Demonstration

We now look at a small program that demonstrates the technique of this section. This program, called *FULLY* (for *Fully* developed system), runs in a Windows Command Console. Complete source code can be found in the FULLY directory, and it includes RAND.CPP for random number generation, PRICE_PERMUTE.CPP for the core permutation classes, and FULLY.CPP as the main program. It is called with three parameters:

```
FULLY   Ntrain   Nreps   MarketFile
```

The *Ntrain* parameter specifies how many prices at the beginning of the market history are used to train the trading system. The *Nreps* parameter specifies how many replications are to be done, including the original, unpermuted run. The *MarketFile* parameter specifies the market history file, each of whose lines specifies the date as YYYYMMDD, the open, high, low, and close. Anything after these prices, such as volume, is ignored. Spaces, tabs, or commas may be used as delimiters. Here are two sample lines from a market history file:

```
19880211 122.32 122.89 121.42 121.92 4015
19880212 121.92 123.37 121.82 122.72 3544
```

The trading system used in this example program is the same trivial moving-average-crossover system used in the OVERFIT example; see the discussion on Page 49 for a review if needed. I won't waste space by showing it again here, although I will note that this implementation includes a subroutine that executes the trained trading system across a specified range of market history. The calling parameters for this system execution routine are as follows:

```
double execute (        // Returns profit factor
   int nprices ,        // Number of log prices in X
   int istart ,         // First trade decision is made on this price index
   double *prices ,     // Log prices
   int short_term ,     // Short-term lookback
   int long_term        // Long-term lookback
   )
```

The caller specifies the total number of prices in the market history as well as the index at which to start computing the performance criterion. This again is the profit factor computed using the supplied prices array, which usually will be the log of the raw prices. The caller must also specify the short-term and long-term lookbacks that have already been optimized over a presumably earlier training period. Note that istart should point to the price immediately *prior* to the OOS test period, because this is the price on which the trade decision is made, with the profit/loss taking place on the first price in the OOS test period.

I'll skip over all of the mundane market-reading code, which you can find in FULLY.CPP. The interesting part starts with 'developing' the final trading system, which here just amounts to optimizing the lookbacks over the user-specified number of initial prices. The opt_params() routine here is essentially identical to that seen in the prior section (Page 49). We use the user-specified ntrain initial prices to find the optimal lookbacks, and optionally provide them to the user. The call to execute() here is completely unnecessary, and is just cheap insurance that may detect programming errors in the opt_params() or execute() routine. It executes the system over the same market history period that was used to train the system, so it had better return exactly the same profit factor. Note that we begin execution at index opt_long-1. Please look back at Figure 3.1 on Page 55 to see that this is the index labeled "First legal decision". This is the first price at which we have enough prices to compute the long-term moving average.

```
opt_return = opt_params ( ntrain , close , &opt_short , &opt_long ) ;
// Optionally print the optimal profit factor and lookbacks here

opt_return = execute ( ntrain , opt_long-1 , close , opt_short , opt_long ) ;
// Optionally verify or print the profit factor to confirm it is the same
```

We now perform the permutation test on the OOS period, those prices beyond the training period. We loop through all user-specified replications. If this is the first, unpermuted run we allocate a new BarPermute object. As in the prior example, our trading system uses only closing prices, so it would be more efficient to just do price permutation. But I permute bars here to make it easier for the reader to drop in his or her own trading system that may require bars. Notice that as discussed earlier we specify the baseline permutation bar as index ntrain-1, the last price in the training period. We also call execute() starting at this index to get the OOS profit factor, an unbiased (if we have never used this OOS period before!) estimate of our trading system's performance. And initialize the counter. If this is not familiar, please review the prior example that starts on Page 49.

If we are past the first replication, permute the prices and call execute() again. If the performance equals or exceeds that of the original run, increment the counter. Finally, we compute the p-value.

```
for (irep=0 ; irep<nreps ; irep++) {

  if (irep == 0) {
    bp_ptr = new BarPermute ( nprices , 1 , ntrain-1 , &open , &high , &low , &close ) ;
    original = execute ( nprices , ntrain-1 , close , opt_short , opt_long ) ;
    // Optionally print unpermuted OOS profit factor here
    count = 1 ;
  }

  else {
    bp_ptr->do_permute () ;
    opt_return = execute ( nprices , ntrain-1 , close , opt_short , opt_long ) ;
    if (opt_return >= original)
      ++count ;
  }
}

pval = (double) count / (double) nreps ) ;
```

I ran this program on several decades of OEX using what most people would call reasonable parameters and got the following unsurprising result:

8021 prices were read. Training with the first 7000...
Profit factor based on log prices = 1.09197
optimal long lookback = 218 short lookback = 32
OOS Profit factor based on log prices = 1.05664
p-value for null hypothesis that OOS performance is worthless = 0.5700

I had somewhat over 8000 price bars and used the first 7000 to 'develop' the trading system. The optimal profit factor in these first 7000 prices was an uninspiring 1.09197. When I went on to test this optimized trading system on the about 1000 remaining OOS prices the profit factor dropped to a dismal 1.05664. And we see that there is more than a 50-50 chance that we could have gotten a result this 'good' from a truly worthless system.

Now here's the interesting and important demonstration, which shows the importance of not being stingy on the data withheld for validation. I raised the training period to 8010, leaving just 11 prices in the OOS period.

8021 prices were read. Training with the first 8010...
Profit factor based on log prices = 1.09170
optimal long lookback = 243 short lookback = 17
OOS Profit factor based on log prices = 1.87414
p-value for null hypothesis that OOS performance is worthless = 0.8400

As expected, the in-sample (optimized over the training period) profit factor and lookbacks don't change much. However, look at that OOS profit factor. It's huge, well up into the truly excellent range. But the p-value is a ridiculously high 0.84, indicating that a truly worthless system could have easily (even likely!) done this well or better in the holdout period.

How did this happen? The tiny OOS period had higher prices than recent history, mostly increasing, resulting in long positions that mostly won. That gave the high profit factor, although due to random 'bad luck' it happened to be low for the circumstances. Permutation preserves trend, so long returns were usually positive, resulting in high profit factors for the permuted runs as well. *This test correctly reported that the excellent OOS profit factor could easily happen without predictive skill, a conclusion that would be missed without a permutation test.* This was exaggerated due to the tiny OOS period, but please understand that great OOS performance can still come from a worthless system. In this case, the large profit factor came from lucky, unusually persistent trend, not intelligence.

Testing a Trading System Factory

I have already presented two specific situations in which a permutation test is valuable. One is when we are in the earliest stage of system development and we want to make sure our system is not vulnerable to overfitting problems. The other is when we have completed development of a trading system and we want to perform a final OOS test. In this section we are looking at a much more general application, a test of the quality of our entire system development process, from the concept of the trading algorithm all the way through our validation process.

But before delving into the main topic of this section, I want to take a moment to pursue the interesting and important demonstration that concluded the prior section, as it is closely related to the current topic.

It is well known (despite not always being strictly true!) that out-of-sample test results are unbiased. In other words, suppose we develop a trading system based on some historical dataset, and then we test the system on more recent data that did not take part in any way in the development process. Under fairly general conditions, and as long as we are somewhat loose in our definition of *unbiased*, we can usually state that the performance result we get from the OOS data is an unbiased estimate of the true expected future performance of the trading system. (We conveniently ignore concerns such as stationarity, distribution anomalies of the criterion, and so forth.)

But here's the vital point. Developers often make the serious mistake of believing that the OOS trades and their implied performance figures(s) are representative of what we will see in the future from this system. Even ignoring the items mentioned at the end of the prior paragraph, even in the most ideal conditions, this is not the case. It is virtually guaranteed that the OOS trades will be either overly optimistic or overly pessimistic. *There is virtually zero probability that they will be truly representative of what we will see from this sytem in the future.*

So then what does *unbiased* really mean? All it means is that, in a mathematical sense best left undefined in this text, neither optimism nor pessimism will be consistently favored. One is as likely as the other. But one or the other is guaranteed!

We saw a vivid example of this at the end of the prior section. We trained a trading system using most of our available historical data and then tested it on a ridiculously short set of OOS data at the end. The profit factor was phenomenal, the sort of profit factor that could make one rich quickly. And *this incredible profit factor is unbiased, because it came from out-of-sample data!*

That should make the reader sit up and take notice, as it's a striking example of how an unbiased performance figure can be far from an accurate estimate of expected future performance. All the fact that it's unbiased means is that it's just as likely that we could have gotten an utterly abysmal profit factor. In this case, the end of the training period had a strong up trend, and that trend continued into and throughout the OOS test period. If instead the price pattern in the OOS period had been antithetical to this trading system we would have gotten a horrid profit factor, with nearly every trade losing money.

This sort of effect is more likely to happen when we have a short OOS time period, which is why we often use walkforward analysis to produce a large number of OOS trades that can be pooled to compute a single performance figure that is relatively stable. But even then our performance criterion is, in the most literal sense, a random variable that almost certainly is an incorrect representation of expected future performance. This is the value of a permutation test on OOS performance. It lets us quantify the likely distribution of performance results that result from worthless systems so we can see if our obtained OOS result stands out from the pack. The example at the end of the prior section showed how the OOS profit factor, though unbiased and excellent, did not stand out from the pack in a permutation test.

What is a Trading System Factory?

When we develop a trading system, we usually go through the following process. I'm not claiming that this is the ideal process; sometimes a shortcut or two might be acceptable, and more often a bit more sophistication is called for. But if one were to survey system developers and ask about their usual process, we would likely end up with a composite that looks something like this:

1) Formulate a general idea of how the market operates and thereby conceive of a general algorithm for taking advantage of this known pattern to predict future market movement. For example, we might decide that trends are persistent and that the value of a short-term moving average relative to a longer-term moving average is a good indicator of trend.

2) Decide how we will take our general concept of a trading system to a specific, rigorously defined trading system. In this step we will decide which parameters we will vary in an effort to maximize performance, and we will choose an optimization algorithm for finding the best parameters.

3) Optimize the system on some old data (we save more recent data for OOS testing) and confirm that performance is excellent. This in-sample performance figure will be optimistically biased, so it had better be excellent. If not, go back to the drawing board. The testing algorithm of this section assumes that this test passes. If it does not, our permutation test will detect poor performance, so we need not worry about this test here.

4) If we're smart, at this point we will employ the overfitting test described on Page 42 and abort if it fails. If we do not perform the overfitting test as part of this system-factory test (and we don't here) it's not a problem because the factory test reports poor performance if the overfitting test would have failed. But in real life you really should do the overfit test to avoid wasting valuable OOS data.

5) We perform a walkforward test. For each fold we re-optimize the trading system's parameters before testing the optimized system on a batch of OOS data that immediately follows the training set, the market period on which the system was optimized. By continually re-optimizing, we enable the system to adapt to changing market conditions. By using walkforward instead of a single hold-out batch of recent data (which we did on Page 54) we maximize the number of OOS trades that we can accumulate for more accurate results.

We can now explore the concept of a trading system factory in the context of this section. It consists of the following components:

1) A general algorithm (not fully specified) for examining past market data and choosing a position (long/short/neutral) to take.

2) An algorithm for finding the specific version of the general trading algorithm that optimizes some measure of performance.

3) The exact specifications of a walkforward algorithm that re-optimizes the trading system and tests it on subsequent OOS data. We must specify the market history to be tested, the number of prices in each training set (the period over which the system is optimized), and the number of OOS prices tested in each walkforward fold.

4) Our measure of performance which is computed from the pooled OOS trades and which we use to evaluate the quality of the trading system.

Why would we want to evaluate the quality of such a trading system factory? The answer is important, because it gets at a vital concept in trading system development. Consider the following quandary: *We nearly always want to optimize our trading system using the most recent data available so as to incorporate current market behavior, but that means that we have no OOS data on which to test our trading system before deploying it.*

As a result, what we generally do is test the trading system factory that produced the system. If we conclude that it is a reliable factory, then we trust the model it produces, retrain the model with the most recent data, and deploy it without further testing.

Permutation Considerations

There are several things that we must consider when we decide how to permute the market history in a way that will destroy predictable patterns without introducing problematic artifacts.

1) The OOS trade returns computed from the original, unpermuted run will be based on those market price changes from the first change in the first OOS fold through the last price change in the dataset. Changes within the training period for the first fold will never play a role in the original OOS trades. Thus, however we permute, we must ensure that changes within the first training set never make it into the OOS area as a result of permutation. This way we keep any unusual changes (very large increases or decreases, or a preponderance of one direction of changes) out of the permuted OOS area where they may distort results, making permuted criteria non-commensurate with the original criterion.

2) Because in the original, unpermuted walkforward we will be re-optimizing the trading system for each fold, we want to be sure that the data on which we are optimizing is permuted for every fold, thus placing the original and permuted runs on equal footing. It would be of questionable validity to re-optimize permutation runs using some or all of the original, unpremuted data.

3) An algorithm that would satisfy those conditions, perhaps be desirable under some limited circumstances, but which I do not illustrate here would be as follows: Permute the initial training data (the market history over which the system is optimized for the first walkforward fold) as an independent unit. Also permute the data in the first walkforward fold as an independent unit. From then on, as you advance the folds, permute only the OOS data for that fold. The advantage of this approach is that nonstationarity, such as unnaturally extended trends or volatility regimes, would be preserved in the permutations for each fold, even though predictable patterns are destroyed. This is good. The disadvantage is that in order to get a usable number of permutations the size of each OOS fold must be large, certainly at least 500 prices. Small OOS folds are precluded.

4) The algorithm that I recommend, use, and present later is as follows:
    Permute the first fold's training set as a single unit, and separately
    permute all of the remaining data as a single unit. Then just perform
    the walkforward as usual. That pair of permutations is sufficient for
    an entire walkforward analysis of a permutation run. This certainly
    satisfies the first two considerations above. There is one clear
    advantage to this method, and one arguable advantage (or some might
    say disadvantage). The advantage is that an enormous number of
    permutations are theoretically possible, even if you use OOS folds as
    small as a single price (which is not unreasonable if computation
    resources allow). This eliminates any problems that can arise from
    having too few different permutations possible. What I see as an
    advantage over the prior method is that market patterns such as
    trends and volatility regimes tend to be diversified across
    permutations, making the permutation runs more to the tune of 'we
    don't know what's coming in the market'. Some people might argue
    that real markets do have unusual periods, so we should not preclude
    this possibility in the permutations. Actually, my considered opinion
    is that it really doesn't matter much one way or the other. This is my
    method, and I'm sticking with it. :)

A Demonstration Program

The folder FACTORY contains three routines. RAND.CPP is a random
number generator. PRICE_PERMUTE.CPP contains the core permutation
routines. And FACTORY.CPP is a program that demonstrates how to test
a trading system factory. It is called with four parameters:

```
FACTORY   Ntrain   Ntest   Nreps   MarketFile
```

The *Ntrain* parameter specifies how many prices at the beginning of the
market history as well as successive training folds are used to train the
trading system. The *Ntest* parameter specifies the number of prices in each
OOS fold, although the last OOS fold may have fewer prices if the market
history runs out. The *Nreps* parameter specifies how many replications are
to be done, including the original, unpermuted run. The *MarketFile*
parameter specifies the market history file, each of whose lines specifies

the date as YYYYMMDD, the open, high, low, and close. Anything after these prices, such as volume, is ignored. Spaces, tabs, or commas may be used as delimiters. Here are two sample lines from a market history file:

```
19880211 122.32 122.89 121.42 121.92 4015
19880212 121.92 123.37 121.82 122.72 3544
```

The trading system used in this example program is the same trivial moving-average-crossover system used in the OVERFIT example; see the discussion on Page 49 for a review if needed. I won't waste space by showing it again here, although I will note that this implementation includes a subroutine that executes the trained trading system across a specified range of market history. The calling parameters for this system execution routine are as follows:

```
void execute (          // Returns profit factor
  int nprices ,          // Number of log prices in X
  int istart ,           // First trade decision is made on this price index
  double *prices ,       // Log prices
  int short_term ,       // Short-term lookback
  int long_term ,        // Long-term lookback
  double *win_sum ,      // Cumulates on top of input value
  double *lose_sum
  )
```

The caller specifies the total number of prices in the market history as well as the index at which to start computing the trades returns. They are computed using the supplied **prices** array, which usually will be the log of the raw prices. The caller must also specify the short-term and long-term lookbacks that have already been optimized over an earlier training period. Note that **istart** should point to the price immediately *prior* to the OOS test period, because this is the price on which the trade decision is made, with the profit/loss taking place on the first price in the OOS test period. The **win_sum** and **lose_sum** parameters cumulate the sum of winning and losing trades, respectively. In a walkforward situation, these would be initialized to zero before the first time **execute()** is called. After the completion of all walkforward folds these quantities will summarize the pooled OOS periods.

I'll skip all the mundane details involved with reading the market data. Note that I use bar permutation, even though this trading algorithm uses only closing prices. This is to make things easier for the reader if he or she wants to drop in their own trading system to replace my crude system. We'll jump right to the interesting part.

The main computation loop makes **nreps** passes, with the first being the unpermuted run that computes the pooled OOS profit factor. Each pass has three blocks of code, shown here. More detailed explanations are interspersed with the listing.

1) On the first pass create the permutation objects but do not permute. On subsequent passes permute the data.
2) Do the walkforward and compute the pooled OOS performance criterion.
3) On the first pass, compute and save the original criterion and initialize the counter to 1. On subsequent passes, increment the counter if a permuted criterion equals or exceeds the original.

```
for (irep=0 ; irep<nreps ; irep++) {
  if (irep == 0) {        // On first pass create objects but do not permute
    tset_bp_ptr = new BarPermute ( ntrain , 1 , 0 , &open , &high , &low , &close ) ;
    oos_bp_ptr = new BarPermute ( nprices , 1 , ntrain-1 , &open , &high , &low ,
                                  &close ) ;
  }
  else {                  // Permute on subsequent passes
    tset_bp_ptr->do_permute () ;  // Initial training set
    oos_bp_ptr->do_permute () ;  // Entire OOS period for all folds
  }
```

On the first pass we allocate the two permutation objects. The training set permutation object contains **ntrain** objects and starts at index 0. The OOS permutation object encompasses all **nprices** prices in the market history, but its base price is at index **ntrain-1**, the last price in the training period. As has been explained earlier, we always set the base price immediately prior to the OOS segment so that the first *change* is out-of-sample.

We now perform the walkforward. For each fold, **tset_start** points to the first price in the training set and **oos_start** points to the first price in the OOS area. Note that we will call **execute()** with a starting price pointed to by oos_start-1 because we need this parameter to point to the first *decision* made for OOS testing; the actual result of that decision, the price change from the decision price to the next price, happens at the beginning of the OOS area.

For all folds except (usually) the last, the number of prices in the OOS test area, n_oos, will be the user-specified ntest. But the price history may run out in the last fold, requiring us to reduce n_oos. The current training fold begins at close+tset_start and contains ntrain prices. The total number of prices from the first through the end of the current OOS area is oos_start+n_oos, and our first OOS decision price is at index oos_start-1. To advance to the next fold we move both starting points ahead by ntest. Finally, do the usual initialization, counting, and p-value computation.

```
tset_start = 0 ;          // Start of current fold's training set
oos_start = ntrain ;      // First decision is 1 bar before oos_start
win_sum = lose_sum = 1.e-60 ; // Cumulates for profit factor
while (1) {
  n_oos = ntest ;                       // Will be this until perhaps last fold
  if (oos_start + n_oos > nprices)      // Is last fold smaller?
    n_oos = nprices - oos_start ;       // Take what's left
  if (n_oos <= 0)                       // Signals that we are done
    break ;
  opt_params ( ntrain , close + tset_start , &opt_short , &opt_long ) ;
  execute ( oos_start + n_oos , oos_start-1 , close , opt_short , opt_long ,
         &win_sum , &lose_sum ) ;
  tset_start += ntest ;
  oos_start += ntest ;
  }

if (irep == 0) {
  original = win_sum / lose_sum ;
  count = 1 ;
  printf ( "\nOOS Profit factor based on log prices = %.5lf\n", original ) ;
  }
else {
  if (win_sum / lose_sum >= original)
    ++count ;
  }
}
pval = (double) count / (double) nreps ) ;
```

Just to make sure the reader fully understands the actions of this program, and the actions that you should perform to validate your own model factory, please examine Figure 3.2 below. This shows a tiny example, having just 10 prices, with the user specifying that the training set contains 5 prices and the OOS test set contains 2 prices. The first fold's training set has price indices 0 through 4, with the OOS test being price indices 5 and 6. For the first OOS test, the first decision price will be at index 4 so that the first profit/loss is obtained from the price at index 5. The second fold moves these time periods 2 prices (ntest) forward. The third fold moves them again, but we reach the end of the data, so the last OOS test period contains only 1 price, index 9.

When we permute, we do so with two independent price sets. One price set is the first training set, indices 0 through 4. The other is all other prices, with the base price (which does not change) being the price immediately prior to the first OOS test period. This base price for permutation is at index 4.

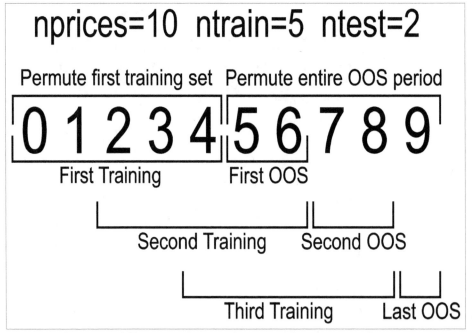

Figure 3.2 Permutation testing a trading system factory

The Demonstration Program In Action

I ran the FACTORY program on OEX from early 1988 through 2019, using a training-set size of 4000 bars and a test-set size of 252 bars, approximately a year. The following results were obtained:

```
OOS Profit factor based on log prices = 1.03455

p-value for null hypothesis that OOS performance is worthless
= 0.270
```

Obviously, the moving-average-crossover system employed here is nearly worthless. The OOS profit factor is pitiful, and there is a 0.27 probability that this could have been attained by sheer luck.

Evaluating Indicators

Before digging into the topic of this section, I want to be clear about the generality of this material. Variables here will be called indicators, but they need not fit the developer's usual idea of an indicator. Perhaps you have a complex nonlinear model that considers numerous traditional indicators and predicts the near-term movement of the market, or the likely profitability of a certain type of trade. For the applications in this section, the output of such a model could be considered an 'indicator'. Or perhaps you don't have a model-based trading system, but rather an algorithmic system that simply flags the position it wants to take. You could code its decisions as +1 for long, –1 for short, and 0 for neutral, and call that an 'indicator'. In other words, *the algorithms presented in this section, while primarily intended to screen and evaluate the performance of traditional indicators, can be applied to any continuous or discrete variables whose value the developer feels might provide information about future market movement.* So for the remainder of this section, any time you see the word 'indicator' you should think 'or predictive model output, or trading system decision'.

One huge conundrum that faces most trading system designers is the selection of suitable indicators for implementing the designer's idea. For example, suppose you are designing a trend-following system. What is the primary indicator you should employ for defining trend? A simple moving-average difference, such as short-term MA minus long-term MA? RSI? Stochastic? MACD? Linear trend? And how far back do you look? A few days? A month? A year?

Another possibility is that you don't even have an idea for a trading system, but you want to do some spaghetti tossing to see what sticks to the wall. Maybe you've come up with a bunch of novel indicator ideas and you want to see if any of your indicators appear to have predictive power. If you have, say, 10 indicator ideas, with 10 trial lookbacks for each, you have 100 indicators to test.

Yet another possibility is that you and perhaps your colleagues have designed and optimized several predictive models for trading systems. Maybe these competing models are based on different indicators, or maybe they have different architectures or hyperparameters. The techniques of this section *cannot* be used to test them on the same dataset on which they were trained; training bias will guarantee that they will appear to be great. But if you have an out-of-sample dataset, a time period that played no role in developing the models, you can execute the models on this OOS dataset and employ the techniques of this section on their OOS predictions.

Regardless of where your variables (which we henceforth call *indicators*) came from, there is a problem that you face, whether you know it or not. Even if every indicator is absolutely worthless, unable to provide any power to predict future market movement, some of them will be lucky just by random chance, and their measured predictive power will be unjustifiably optimistic. In fact, if you have more than a few competitors, it is virtually guaranteed that at least one of them will show outstanding performance, an apparently excellent indicator despite being in fact worthless. In my experience, the vast majority of trading system developers greatly underestimate the power of luck. So the primary goal of this section will be to present a permutation test that lets us estimate the probability that any outstanding performance that we observed could have been due to nothing more than good luck.

Measuring Future Market Movement

For each time slot at which we have values of our indicators we will also have a measured value of future market price movement. As I've stated previously in this book, in order for a permutation test (or nearly any other statistical test) to provide valid results, it is crucial that the market returns that take part in the test have negligible serial correlation. As I've also previously stated, when computing profit factor (my preferred performance criterion) from market returns, it is important to do so at the highest resolution possible. These two facts tell us that we should not pool multiple future market changes into single multiple-bar changes. For example, if we are interested in working with day bars, we should not measure indicators every day but then use the total return over the next three days as our measure of market movement. If we did so, adjacent market movement measures would have two out of three days in common, resulting in huge serial correlation. The market change over the next day would have the highest resolution possible and have negligible serial correlation.

In most applications, at least at the indicator-screening stage, using the next day's (bar's) return is ideal. The predictive power of indicators generally peaks immediately after they are measured and drops fairly rapidly after that, so measuring the next bar's return is a great way to detect predictive power. But if for some reason you really want to consider multiple-bar returns, you have several options. You could skip through the market history at whatever lookahead distance you desire. For example, if you want a three-bar return you could measure the indicators and return every third bar, which eliminates serial correlation by eliminating overlap. Alternatively, under the nearly always valid assumption that indicator values do not change significantly over a reasonably short lookahead distance, you could just mark the position to market every day, generating a separate (and uncorrelated) series of the components of the multiple-bar return. One of these two methods will nearly always be fine, and honestly, in my experience neither is ever even necessary. Associating indicator values with the return over the next bar is nearly always the best way to measure their predictive power.

There is one small modification to using the market return that I have found to be beneficial in most cases. A given market move's importance can be thought of as being relative to the market volatility at the time. A given market move during a time of high market volatility may be insignificant, while that same move may be large in a period of small volatility. In fact, many traders will adjust the size of their positions according to market volatility. So I find that the best measure of market return is to first compute the change as the difference in log of prices (or equivalently, the log of the ratio of prices). Then I measure the average true range (ATR) over a suitable lookback, typically several months to a year. I divide the market change by the ATR to get my final measure of market change for the tests in this section. This seems to work well for me, and I recommend it.

Measuring Predictive Power

In general data-mining applications there are many good choices for associating one quantity (an indicator value here) with another quantity (future market movement here). Mutual information is good, and uncertainty reduction is usually even better; both of these are described in some of my prior books and numerous references can be found online. However, for financial market trading applications my preferred measure is the profit factor obtained by optimal high and/or low thresholds.

Let us assume that our indicator is not negatively correlated with future market movement; in case we find that it is we can simply flip its sign for the purposes of this discussion. Then we can do one or both of two things to measure its predictive power. We can find a high threshold that maximizes the profit factor obtained by taking a long position whenever the indicator equals or exceeds this threshold. We can also find a low threshold that maximizes the profit factor obtained by taking a short position whenever the indicator is strictly less than this threshold. If we have a preconceived notion of what sort of predictability we most desire, we can look at just one of these measures. More generally, we can consider the greater of the two profit factors. We never want to pool the returns into a combined long+short 'trading system' because that would penalize an indicator that did well on one side but poorly on the other, a very common situation. This is why if we have no preference for long or short predictability we should use the maximum of the two as our measure of predictive power.

There are two issues to be aware of with this way of measuring predictive power. First, profit factor is seriously unstable when there are just a few returns going into the calculation. Thus, we should require that at least a specified minimum number of cases satisfy each threshold. I recommend at least 100. The other issue is that the process of optimizing the threshold to maximize the profit factor introduces significant optimistic bias. Even completely worthless indicators will show predictive power after optimization. The testing algorithms described in this section fully account for this optimization bias, but you must not be fooled when you see surprisingly high profit factors. They are inflated.

Permutation Test for Selection Bias

There are two sections that I would like you to review before continuing in this section. First, please reread the overview of the Monte-Carlo permutation test that begins on Page 10. Then examine the short code listing for overfit testing that is on Page 52 and make sure you understand how these two items relate.

Let's take a moment to discuss selection bias. Everyone knows (or should know) that *training bias* is the optimistic performance bias that happens when a trading system has its parameters optimized. But there is another, more subtle form of bias that shows up in trading system development. Suppose we have two or more competing trading systems or individual indicators and we select whichever among the competitors shows the best performance. If the performance comparison was done on truly out-of-sample data, it is tempting to think that the performances of the competitors, including that of the best, are all unbiased. Indeed, if we were to look at just one of them in isolation, this would be true. So, for example, suppose there was no competition; our only indicator or trading system was the one that happens to be best among some hypothetical universe of competitors. We just run that one OOS test and examine that one performance figure. Then that performance is unbiased. But as soon as we run a competition and pick the best, the performance of that best competitor is no longer unbiased.

This may seem counter-intuitive. Suppose we test *A* and *B* on OOS data and get a performance figure for each. Those two performance figures are each unbiased. But suppose our plan is to choose the better competitor, and suppose it happens to be *A*. Suddenly, the performance of *A* is no longer unbiased; it has an optimistic bias. How can this be? One moment *A*'s performance is unbiased, and the next moment it is biased.

The answer is that after choosing the best, even though it happened to be *A*, the performance figure we are looking at is no longer that of *A*. Rather it is the performance of *The Best*. That is something else entirely. Even though *The Best* happens to be *A*, they are still different. The selection of *The Best* happened in the context of also examining *B* and selecting it if its performance were better.

Looking into this issue a little more deeply, consider the fact that the measured performance of each competitor consists of two components, true predictive power, and luck, which may be good or bad. If there were no luck involved there would be no selection bias. But when we select the best competitor, we are not comparing just true predictive power. We are also comparing luck. Thus, unless their true power is very different, we will have a strong inclination to pick the *luckiest* of the competitors. And of course, in real life luck does not hold. So by favoring the luckiest competitor, we are also inclined to choose the competitor most likely to suffer performance deterioration when its good luck fails. This is the source of our selection bias, and we will now develop a permutation algorithm that accounts for this.

I trust that you have reviewed the two items mentioned at the start of this section. I now state the basic Monte-Carlo permutation test as exemplified in those two readings. The user specifies a number of replications nreps, which includes the original, unpermuted replication.

```
For irep from 0 through nreps-1
   if irep > 0
      shuffle

   compute the criterion

   if irep=0
      original_criterion = criterion
      count = 1

   else
      if criterion >= original_criterion
         count = count + 1

p-value = count / nreps
```

Please make sure you understand this algorithm, as it is the foundation on which the more complex selection bias algorithm is based. The p-value computed this way is often called the *solo p-value* because it refers to a single (solo) test, considered in isolation. This is in contrast to the p-value that we will soon compute, often called the *unbiased p-value*. It is called this because it accounts for selection bias by looking at each candidate indicator in the context of the complete set of competing indicators.

The unbiased p-value is computed by an extension of the solo algorithm. Consider the following simple extension that is almost but not quite what we will do. Suppose we examine the original, unpermuted criterion for each competing indicator and select the largest criterion from among them. We can then compute the probability that, if all competitors were worthless, the largest that we observed could have arisen by good luck alone. All we do is, for each permutation, find the largest criterion among the competitors and increment our counter if this permuted maximum equals or exceeds the original maximum. The final count divided by the number of replications is the unbiased p-value for the winner. But we will extend this algorithm in one small but useful way as shown below:

```
For irep from 0 through nreps-1
   if irep > 0
      shuffle

   for ivar from 0 through n_indicators-1
      compute criterion[ivar]

      if irep=0
         original_criterion[ivar] = criterion[ivar]
         solo_count[ivar] = 1
         unbiased_count[ivar] = 1

      else
         if criterion[ivar] >= original_criterion[ivar]
            solo_count[ivar] = solo_count[ivar] + 1

   if irep > 0
      best_criterion = MAX [criterion of all indicators]
      for ivar from 0 through n_indicators-1
         if best_criterion >= original_criterion[ivar]
            unbiased_count[ivar] = unbiased_count[ivar] + 1

for ivar from 0 through n_indicators-1
   solo p-value[ivar] = solo_count[ivar] / nreps
   unbiased p-value[ivar] = unbiased_count[ivar] / nreps
```

There are three things to notice about this algorithm:
1) The solo p-value is computed in exactly the same way as in the basic algorithm shown earlier.
2) For whichever competitor has the largest criterion, its unbiased p-value is computed by a direct extension of the basic algorithm, comparing the original max to the max of each permutation.
3) For competitors with lesser criteria, the meaning of the unbiased p-value is not immediately clear but is now explained.

The exact mathematics behind the unbiased p-value for competitors other than that having the maximum criterion is too deep to consider here, so I will just state the bottom line: *The unbiased p-value computed as shown here is an **upper bound** on the true p-value for that rank-ordered indicator.* For example, consider the indicator having the second-largest criterion. Under the null hypothesis that all competitors are worthless, there is some unknown probability that the second-largest observed criterion could have been at least as large as we obtained by just good luck. The unbiased p-value computed with the algorithm just shown is an upper bound for this unknown true p-value. (On Page 90 we will explore an alternative experimental algorithm that is superior in most ways.)

This 'upper bound' issue is not as much of a problem as one might suspect. We cannot interpret a large p-value as evidence that the indicator is worthless, but doing so would be perilously close to illegally accepting a null hypothesis anyway. So we lose very little on that end. And since the computed p-value is an upper bound on the true p-value, if we obtain a small p-value we can treat that as evidence of the quality of that indicator, since the true p-value is likely even smaller and certainly no larger.

The code that will be shown soon implements this algorithm, but in a slightly different order. Here is the algorithm; a short discussion follows.

```
for ivar from 0 through n_indicators-1
   compute and print original_criterion[ivar]

for ivar from 0 through n_indicators-1
   solo_count[ivar] = unbiased_count[ivar] = 1

for nreps-1 replications
   permute target
   for ivar from 0 through n_indicators-1
      compute criterion[ivar]
      if criterion[ivar] >= original_criterion[ivar]
         solo_count[ivar] = solo_count[ivar] + 1
   max_criterion = MAX (criterion[ivar], ivar=0,...)
   for ivar from 0 through n_indicators-1
      if max_criterion >= original_criterion[ivar]
         unbiased_count[ivar] = unbiased_count[ivar] + 1

for ivar from 0 through n_indicators-1
   solo_pval[ivar] = solo_count[ivar] / nreps
   unbiased_pval[ivar] = unbiased_count[ivar] / nreps
```

If you do not see how this algorithm is identical to the prior algorithm, please study them until it becomes clear. I just revised the order of operations, computing all original criteria first. This lets the program easily and clearly print the optimal criteria before commencing the permutations, rather than computing them in the first 'permutation'.

A Program to Perform the Permutation Test

The directory INDICATOR contains the following files:
    IND.CPP - The main program for performing indicator analysis
    RAND.CPP - Random number generator
    QSORTD.CPP - Sorting algorithms
    SPEARMAN.CPP - Compute Spearman rho nonparametric correlation
    READFILE.CPP - Read a standard database file

The program is called with four parameters:

```
IND   Floor   Nreps   DataFile   ControlFile
```

The *Floor* parameter specifies a fraction that is at most 0.5 and typically about 0.1. When the optimal threshold for profit factor is found, at least this fraction of cases must satisfy the threshold. The *Nreps* parameter specifies how many replications are to be done, including the original, unpermuted run. The *DataFile* parameter specifies the database file that supplies all indicator and target values. The first line of the database file contains all of the variable names. Variable names must be separated by spaces, tabs, or commas, and names must consist of only letters, numbers, and the underscore character (_). Case (upper or lower) is ignored, and all letters will be treated as upper case. Successive lines contain cases, one per case. Here is an example of the first few lines of a typical database file.

```
CMMA_5 CMMA_20 LIN_5 LIN_20 RSI_5 RSI_20 STO_5 STO_20 DAY_RETURN
 -7.8488   1.0718   0.1133   2.3281  44.4571  60.4174  55.6122  69.2106   0.9557
 21.8605  14.6568   2.4180   2.6903  74.1705  66.1461  66.7988  76.8624   0.3803
```

The control file is a text file that lists variable names that appeared in the database file, one name per line. The first name is the target, the variable that specifies future market movement. Subsequent lines name the indicator candidates, a subset of the variables named in the database file. If a variable appears in the control file that did not appear in the database file, an error will be generated. Here is a typical control file:

```
DAY_RETURN
CMMA_5
CMMA_20
LIN_5
LIN_20
RSI_5
RSI_20
STO_5
STO_20
```

Code For the Permutation Test

On Page 79 we saw the permutation test algorithm for accounting not only for training bias but selection bias as well. We now present the code, extracted from IND.CPP, that implements this test. The algorithm as shown was concerned with just one performance measure, but this code will apply this test to three different performance measures: long trades alone, short trades alone, and whichever type of trade performs best. If the user knows *in advance of performing the test* that he or she will be interested in trading only one side of the market, then the test dedicated to that side is appropriate. However, if the developer is keeping an open mind and is looking for a relationship of either sort between the indicators and the target then the 'best' set of statistics should be used.

The first step is to compute and print the optimized long and short thresholds and their corresponding profit factors, presenting this information in a unified table. This code, shown on the next page, also performs an important task. For each indicator it computes the nonparametric correlation (Spearman rho) between the indicator and the target. If the correlation is negative, it flips the sign of the indicator. This way we can assume that the indicator being above the upper threshold on average corresponds to a positive future return, and vice versa for the lower threshold, greatly simplifying the program as well as user interpretation. In unusual circumstances it can happen that behavior at the extremes is opposite behavior over the full range, in which case this is a severely counterproductive action! If you have reason to believe that your indicator has this rare property you will need to modify the code to avoid this action and guaranty that your supplied indicators have the correct sign. As a convenience for the user, we print (+) or (-) after the indicator name to clearly flag whether the sign was flipped. The criterion routine opt_thresh() will be discussed in the next section.

```
fprintf (fp_log , "\n\nOptimization results...\n" ) ;
fprintf (fp_log , "     Variable     Rho  Long thresh  Long pf  Short thresh  Short pf" );

for (ivar=0 ; ivar<n_indicators ; ivar++) {
   k = ind_index[ivar] ;                    // Column in database of this competitor
   for (i=0 ; i<ncases ; i++)
      ind_work[i] = data[i*nvars+k] ;        // Copy this indicator from database
   rho = spearman ( ncases , ind_work , target_work , dwork1 , dwork2 ) ;

   if (rho < 0.0) { // Make sure that indicator and target are positively correlated
      for (i=0 ; i<ncases ; i++) { // Flip sign of this indicator in database
         data[i*nvars+k] = -data[i*nvars+k] ;
         ind_work[i] = data[i*nvars+k] ;     // Get flipped version from database
         }
      }

   if (rho >= 0.0) // For user, print sign of correlation (redundant but clear)
      fprintf ( fp_log , "\n%15s (+) %6.3lf", names[k], rho ) ;
   else
      fprintf ( fp_log , "\n%15s (-) %6.3lf", names[k], rho ) ;

   opt_thresh ( ncases , (int) (floor * ncases + 0.5) , 0 , ind_work , target_work ,
            &dummy , &long_thresh[ivar] , &original_long_pf[ivar] ,
            &short_thresh[ivar] , &original_short_pf[ivar] , dwork1 , dwork2 ) ;

   fprintf ( fp_log , " %11.4lf %8.3lf  %12.4lf %10.3lf",
            long_thresh[ivar] , original_long_pf[ivar] ,
            short_thresh[ivar] , original_short_pf[ivar] ) ;

   original_best_pf[ivar] = (original_long_pf[ivar] > original_short_pf[ivar]) ?
                      original_long_pf[ivar] : original_short_pf[ivar] ;
   }
```

```
for (ivar=0 ; ivar<n_indicators ; ivar++) {
  long_solo_count[ivar] = long_unbiased_count[ivar] = 1 ;
  short_solo_count[ivar] = short_unbiased_count[ivar] = 1 ;
  best_solo_count[ivar] = best_unbiased_count[ivar] = 1 ;
  }

for (irep=0 ; irep<nreps-1 ; irep++) {
  // Shuffle target
  i = ncases ;     // Number remaining to be shuffled
  while (i > 1) { // While at least 2 left to shuffle
    j = (int) (unifrand() * i) ;
    if (j >= i)     // Cheap insurance against disaster if unifrand() returns 1.0
      j = i - 1 ;
    dummy = target_work[--i] ;
    target_work[i] = target_work[j] ;
    target_work[j] = dummy ;
    }

  for (ivar=0 ; ivar<n_indicators ; ivar++) {
    k = ind_index[ivar] ;                  // Column in database of this indicator
    for (i=0 ; i<ncases ; i++)
      ind_work[i] = data[i*nvars+k] ;      // Fetch it from database
    rho = spearman ( ncases , ind_work , target_work , dwork1 , dwork2 ) ;
    if (rho < 0.0) { // Make sure that indicator and target are positively correlated
      for (i=0 ; i<ncases ; i++)      // Flip sign of this indicator
        ind_work[i] = -ind_work[i] ;
      }
    opt_thresh ( ncases , (int) (floor * ncases + 0.5) , 0 , ind_work , target_work ,
            &dummy , &dummy , &long_pf , &dummy , &short_pf , dwork1 , dwork2 ) ;
    best_pf = (long_pf > short_pf) ? long_pf : short_pf ;
    if (long_pf >= original_long_pf[ivar])
      ++long_solo_count[ivar] ;
    if (short_pf >= original_short_pf[ivar])
      ++short_solo_count[ivar] ;
    if (best_pf >= original_best_pf[ivar])
      ++best_solo_count[ivar] ;
    if (ivar == 0 || long_pf > max_long_pf)        // Keep track of MAX for next step
      max_long_pf = long_pf ;
    if (ivar == 0 || short_pf > max_short_pf)
      max_short_pf = short_pf ;
    if (ivar == 0 || best_pf > max_best_pf)
      max_best_pf = best_pf ;
    }
```

```
    for (ivar=0 ; ivar<n_indicators ; ivar++) {
      if (max_long_pf >= original_long_pf[ivar])
        ++long_unbiased_count[ivar] ;
      if (max_short_pf >= original_short_pf[ivar])
        ++short_unbiased_count[ivar] ;
      if (max_best_pf >= original_best_pf[ivar])
        ++best_unbiased_count[ivar] ;
      }
    } // For irep
```

The code just shown is a straightforward implementation of the algorithm
that was shown on Page 79; please refer back to that algorithm and its two
predecessors if you are unclear on anything.

Optimizing the Threshold

The preceding code called **opt_thresh()** to find the long and short
thresholds that maximize their respective profit factors. We now discuss
that code, which is also found in IND.CPP. The calling parameters are as
follows:

```
void opt_thresh (
  int n ,                    // Number of indicator/return pairs
  int min_kept ,             // Must keep (trade) at least this many cases
  int flip_sign ,            // If nonzero, flip sign of indicator
  double *signal_vals ,      // Indicators
  double *returns ,          // Associated returns
  double *pf_all ,           // Profit factor of entire dataset
  double *high_thresh ,      // Upper threshold, for long trades
  double *pf_high ,          // Profit factor >= threshold
  double *low_thresh ,       // Lower threshold, for short trades
  double *pf_low ,           // Profit factor < threshold
  double *work_signal ,      // Work area n long
  double *work_return        // Work area n long
  )
```

The IND program takes as a user parameter the fraction, typically about 0.1, of cases that must satisfy each threshold. But this routine is given an actual count, so when it is called we just set min_kept to n times that fraction, rounded. The flip_sign parameter here would always be set to zero (do not flip) because the calling program already took care of making sure that the indicators are not negatively correlated with the target. The pf_all parameter returns the profit factor that would be obtained by holding a long position for the entire time. This program does not use this value, but it can be a helpful basis against which to compare optimal profit factors; understand that its reciprocal is the profit factor obtained by holding a short position throughout. This lets you compare optimal values to naive values. The routine also returns the optimal thresholds and their corresponding profit factors.

The first step is to copy the indicator and associated market returns to work areas and then sort the indicators (work_signal) in ascending order. Their associated returns in work_return are moved simultaneously, keeping the indicator and return values correctly paired. Then we initialize by computing the profit factor that would be obtained by being long for the entire period. This implies that the upper (long) threshold is at the threshold defined by the element at best_high_index=0 in the sorted indicators, the smallest indicator value.

```
for (i=0 ; i<n ; i++) {
  work_signal[i] = flip_sign ? (-signal_vals[i]) : signal_vals[i] ;
  work_return[i] = returns[i] ;
  }

qsortds ( 0 , n-1 , work_signal , work_return ) ;

win_above = win_below = lose_above = lose_below = 0.0 ;
for (i=0 ; i<n ; i++) {
  if (work_return[i] > 0.0)        // We are long so this is a win
    win_above += work_return[i] ;
  else
    lose_above -= work_return[i] ;
  }

*pf_all = best_high_pf = win_above / (lose_above + 1.e-30) ;
best_high_index = 0 ;   // Complete set is implied by threshold at smallest value
```

At this time we are using the smallest indicator value as both our upper (long) and lower (short) thresholds, and we have the associated long profit factor in **best_high_pf**. Since short positions are defined by the indicator being strictly less than the threshold (equality is not included), we have no short positions. Work our way up through the sorted indicator values, which increases the threshold as we go. Every time we move up, a single case moves from the long side to the short side. We'll deal with tied indicator values in a moment. In the loop over i below, the indicator value at index **i+1** is the implied threshold (long, which includes equality, and short, which does not).

```
best_low_pf = -1.0 ;
best_low_index = n-1 ;   // This should never be necessary
                         // but it avoids a crash if pathological condition


for (i=0 ; i<n-1 ; i++) {      // Indicator[i+1] is a candidate threshold

  // Remove this case from high (long) set
  if (work_return[i] > 0.0)
    win_above -= work_return[i] ;
  else
    lose_above += work_return[i] ;

  // Add this case to low (short) set
  if (work_return[i] > 0.0)
    lose_below += work_return[i] ;
  else
    win_below -= work_return[i] ;
```

This trial threshold at **i+1** is legitimate only if it is a new value. Subsequent values in a tied block are not new, unique thresholds. So if we have a tie, don't do anything about updating best thresholds; we already did this when we hit the first element in this tied block. So now we just have to move past the tied block and get to the next unique indicator value.

```
  if (work_signal[i+1] == work_signal[i])
    continue ;
```

If we have enough long trades in the 'above' set, see about updating the best high threshold. Make sure we don't divide by zero in rare situations. Update the index in the sorted array of the best high threshold.

```
if (n-i-1 >= min_kept) {
  if (win_above / (lose_above + 1.e-30) > best_high_pf) {
    best_high_pf = win_above / (lose_above + 1.e-30) ;
    best_high_index = i+1 ;
    }
  }
```

Do the same for the low threshold, which controls short trades.

```
if (i+1 >= min_kept) {
  if (win_below / (lose_below + 1.e-30) > best_low_pf) {
    best_low_pf = win_below / (lose_below + 1.e-30) ;
    best_low_index = i+1 ;
    }
  }
} // For all trial thresholds
```

That's it. Return the essential results to the caller.

```
*high_thresh = work_signal[best_high_index] ;
*low_thresh = work_signal[best_low_index] ;
*pf_high = best_high_pf ;
*pf_low = best_low_pf ;
}
```

An Example Application

I computed a set of indicators and a target for OEX from early 1988 through the end of 2019. These are as follows:

DAY_RETURN - Next day log return divided by 252-day average true range for volatility normalization.
CMMA_N - Current close minus N-day moving average, scaled and normalized.
LIN_ATR_N - Linear trend over the prior N days, normalized by 252-day average true range.
RSI_N - Ordinary RSI with N-day lookback
LINDEV_N - Current close's deviation from its value predicted by linear projection over the prior N days, suitably normalized.
PVFIT_N - Price-volume fit over the prior N days.
RTVY_N - Reactivity computed over the prior N days.

If you are interested in exactly how these indicators were computed, they are discussed in detail in my book "Statistically Sound Indicators for Financial Market Prediction".

I ran the IND program using the DAY_RETURN target and these indicators computed with several lookbacks, and with 1000 replications. The optimal thresholds and profit factors are as follows:

Variable		Rho	Long thr	Long pf	Short thr	Short pf
CMMA_5	(-)	-0.050	7.7419	1.423	-6.5944	1.017
CMMA_10	(-)	-0.054	9.1368	1.597	-3.9037	0.981
CMMA_20	(-)	-0.043	12.3398	1.397	-5.5540	0.982
LIN_ATR_5	(-)	-0.036	24.7723	1.303	-19.7236	0.988
LIN_ATR_7	(-)	-0.045	21.4862	1.394	-17.3554	1.026
LIN_ATR_15	(-)	-0.021	15.1428	1.244	-18.2686	0.945
RSI_5	(-)	-0.052	-28.8175	1.544	-71.5579	0.989
RSI_10	(-)	-0.046	-36.1751	1.475	-57.0598	0.978
RSI_20	(-)	-0.036	-41.4523	1.419	-65.5329	1.012
LINDEV_5	(-)	-0.008	26.2327	1.185	-26.9793	0.993
LINDEV_10	(-)	-0.016	33.3522	1.168	-6.8519	0.920
LINDEV_20	(-)	-0.039	32.9259	1.387	-16.3927	0.983
PVFIT_7	(+)	0.001	14.3582	1.279	-17.2509	1.022
PVFIT_15	(-)	-0.010	21.7791	1.178	5.0897	0.924
RTVY_6	(-)	-0.049	16.0264	1.462	-7.1658	0.994
RTVY_12	(-)	-0.029	15.1335	1.228	-13.7269	0.955
RTVY_25	(-)	-0.028	18.7179	1.259	-20.7411	1.027

It's worth noting that all but one of these indicators was negatively correlated with the target. That's all the more interesting because these are all, to some degree, traditionally known as momentum indicators, being based on recent trend. So it appears that, at least for these relatively short lookbacks and looking ahead just one day, that they are signaling counter-trend situations. This is less surprising when one notes that the thresholds are rather extreme. For example, with RSI_5 we take a long position when RSI is less than 28.8 (negative RSI greater than -28.8), a clearly oversold condition.

The solo and unbiased p-values for these indicators, sorted from largest long profit factor to lowest, are as shown below.

```
   Variable   profit factor   solo pval   unbiased pval
    CMMA_10        1.597         0.003         0.006
     RSI_5         1.544         0.003         0.021
    RSI_10         1.475         0.013         0.099
    RTVY_6         1.462         0.006         0.123
    CMMA_5         1.423         0.029         0.235
    RSI_20         1.419         0.025         0.249
   CMMA_20         1.397         0.034         0.336
  LIN_ATR_7        1.394         0.043         0.351
  LINDEV_20        1.387         0.043         0.391
  LIN_ATR_5        1.303         0.167         0.851
    PVFIT_7        1.279         0.273         0.927
   RTVY_25         1.259         0.326         0.964
  LIN_ATR_15       1.244         0.418         0.982
   RTVY_12         1.228         0.523         0.996
  LINDEV_5         1.185         0.780         1.000
  PVFIT_15         1.178         0.823         1.000
  LINDEV_10        1.168         0.881         1.000
```

The unbiased p-values for the two best indicators, CMMA_10 and RSI_5, are clearly outstanding. For CMMA_10, 0.006 is the probability that, if all of our competitors were worthless, the best profit factor among them could have been at least the 1.597 that we observed. I'll hang my hat on that any day. Recall from our earlier discussion that once we go below the single best indicator, all subsequent unbiased p-values are upper bounds for the true p-values. So even the third and possibly the fourth competitors are in contention for being useful. This is reinforced by the fact that their solo p-values, while not taking into account selection bias, are still impressive.

Controlling the Familywise Error Rate

I'll begin by saying that the algorithm described in this section and implemented for the optimal-profit-factor test of the prior section is my own semi-rigorous development, largely based on Romano and Wolf (2016) "Efficient Computation of Adjusted p-Values for Resampling-Based Stepdown Multiple Testing", but not rigorously proved by me. I have, however, run many numerical simulations of many experimental conditions, and in every case the simulation results were completely in accord with the expected theoretical results. Thus, I am reasonably confident that this algorithm is mathematically correct. Also, understand that this algorithm could be implemented for any permutation test of selection bias. I do present the algorithm in its most general form, but my implementation here is directly analogous to the indicator selection test of the prior section, making it easy for the reader to do side-by-side comparisons of algorithms and results.

Why consider this alternative algorithm? The traditional selection-bias algorithm, for all its utility, suffers from two annoying weaknesses:

1) The null hypothesis is that *all* competitors are unrelated to the target. This is a significant restriction, at least theoretically. In practice, this restriction seems to create no apparent ill effect when violated, but it makes me uncomfortable. (If needed, see Page 8 for a brief review of hypothesis tests.)

2) The computed probability is strictly correct only for whichever competitor has the greatest relationship with the target. All other selection-bias p-values are upper bounds on the true probabilities. This fact was discussed in the prior section.

The second problem, while troubling, is not devastating, because all competitors for which the computed p-value is less than or equal to the desired alpha level for the test can be considered to be related to the target. That joint statement should satisfy the alpha level because if the least of those that satisfy alpha does so, then certainly all those superior to it do as well. This statement is rather heuristic and could use some rigor, though I am quite confident in its truth in regard to practical applications.

On the other hand, even this result is not ideal because we could easily miss some competitors that are truly related to the target. If their computed p-values overestimate the true probabilities under the null hypothesis to a degree that causes the computed p-value to exceed alpha, despite there being a relationship with the target, then we have missed this competitor. This loss of power is a significant problem, and the algorithm described in this section largely or completely solves it.

This alternative procedure is much better than the traditional one-shot method of the prior section, which pools all candidates into a single batch with the null hypothesis that they are *all* unrelated to the target. This new method tests each null hypothesis *individually*, but with the *familywise error rate* (*FWE*) controlled by our desired alpha. The FWE is the probability of rejecting one or more of the true individual null hypotheses. More loosely speaking, FWE is the probability of making even one mistake in identifying individual null hypotheses to reject.

FWE comes in two forms. An FWE with weak control is one which requires that all null hypotheses be true. This is what we have in the traditional selection-bias test. Far more desirable is an FWE with strong control, which means that it holds regardless of which or how many of the null hypotheses are true. This, of course, corresponds better to real life. In my own professional work I have always acted as if the traditional selection-bias test has strong control even though it does not, and it's never come back to bite me. Much heuristic evidence supports that use. Still, a method with strong control would be more appealing.

An even more desirable property of a selection-bias test is that it have as much power as possible. In the case of multiple null hypotheses there are many possible definitions of power. At one extreme we might want to maximize the probability of rejecting at least one false null hypothesis. At the other extreme we might want to maximize the probability of rejecting all false null hypotheses. Those are both too extreme, one with too little demanded and one with too much demanded. More reasonably we might want to maximize some measure of average rejection probability. This intermediate goal, perhaps maximizing the average probability of rejecting false null hypotheses, is doubtless the best, and is a property that I believe is possessed by my new algorithm.

We must understand this property of maximum power, because it is very important in practice. Recall that the traditional selection-bias algorithm provides only upper bounds for the p-values for all competitors except the best. This makes it possible that it will fail to reject null hypotheses (decide that there is a relationship) for competitors that truly have a relationship with the target. That's the beauty of this new algorithm: it can often flag competitors that would have been missed by the traditional algorithm due to overestimation of p-values, while still maintaining a user-specified familywise error rate.

In summary, we want to be able to test each *individual* competitor's null hypothesis while having strong control of the FWE and maximizing average power. The traditional selection-bias algorithm has only weak control of the FWE and it has excellent power only for whichever competitor is the best (maximum relationship with the target).

I believe that my new algorithm provides these superior properties. The algorithm will be shown soon. But first I want to discuss the general philosophy of the procedure so as to make the algorithm more clear.

This is a stepwise procedure, with hypotheses being rejected one at a time, in order starting with the best competitor (largest target relationship) and working downward until no more null hypotheses can be rejected at the user-specified FWE, alpha level. As each null hypothesis is tested, we approximate the null-hypothesis distribution of that relationship statistic by permuting the target as in the traditional algorithm, but finding the maximum of *only the competitors that have not yet had their null hypotheses rejected*. This is the critical difference between this improved algorithm and the traditional selection-bias algorithm. If, for each step, we were to approximate the null hypothesis distribution by finding the maximum relationship statistic of all permuted competitors we would have an algorithm that is essentially identical to the traditional algorithm, just re-ordered as stepwise instead of all at once. However, in the new algorithm, the number of competitors that go into the computation of the maximum relationship statistic is reduced by one for each step, thus shrinking the null distribution.

In summary, this algorithm is almost identical to the traditional algorithm, except that instead of testing all null hypotheses at once, we test them one at a time, and as we do successive tests we keep shrinking the number of competing distributions that go into approximating the null distribution.

I'll now walk through the algorithm listed on the next page, and continue the walkthrough after the listing. Note that this algorithm is relatively straightforward and easy to understand, but too slow for practical work. An equivalent but much faster version will be shown in the next section.

The user has specified that there are n competing populations (indicators here), and the test will employ m permutations (thousands) to estimate the null hypothesis distributions. A desired **alpha** level (maximum FWE that the user can accept) for the test has also been specified.

The first step is to compute the relationship statistic for each competitor and store them in the **original** array. We'll also need to sort them so that the stepwise procedure can proceed from best (largest) to smallest. But we must not disturb the order of **original**, so we copy that array to a work array and sort it ascending. We also initialize **sort_indices** to an identity array, and when we do the sorting we simultaneously move the elements of this array. Thus, after sorting, **sort_indices[0]** will be the index of the competitor having the smallest relationship, **sort_indices[1]** the next smallest, and so forth. Later, the stepwise procedure will work backwards through this array to test the populations in order from best to worst.

As competitors have their null hypotheses rejected, we keep track of which have been rejected via the **passed** array, where a TRUE value means that its null hypothesis has been rejected; it passed the test for having a relationship with the target. Prepare for the stepwise accumulation loop by initializing **passed** to FALSE for all competitors.

–> Compute the relationship for each competitor and sort

For i from 0 through n-1
  sort_indices[i] = i ;
  original[i] = relationship of competitor i with Y
  work[i] = original[i] ;

Sort work ascending, moving sort_indices simultaneously

–> Initialize that no competitors have yet passed (null rejected)

For i from 0 through n-1
  passed[i] = FALSE ;

–> The stepwise accumulation loop begins here

For step from n-1 through 0, working backwards (best to worst)
  this_i = sort_indices[step]   *Index of best remaining competitor*
  count[this_i] = 1 ;   *Counts right-tail probability*

  –> Permutation loop estimates null distribution of population

  For irep from 1 through m   *Do all random replications*
    Shuffle Y

    max_f = number smaller than smallest possible relationship
    For i from 0 through n-1
      if (NOT passed[i])   *Do only those without null rejected*
        this_f = relationship of competitor i with Y
        if (this_f > max_f)   *Keep track of maximum*
          max_f = this_f ;

    If (max_f >= original[this_i])
      ++count[this_i] ;   *Count right-tail probability*

  –> See if this new competitor passed (NULL rejected).

  If count[this_i] / (m+1) <= alpha
    passed[this_i] = TRUE
  Else
    Break out of step loop; we are done

The stepwise accumulation loop now begins. It moves backwards through the competing indicators because they have been sorted ascending and we want to begin with the best. Recall that **sort_indices** contains the indices of the sorted competitors, so we place in this_i the index of the competitor that is about to be tested for inclusion in the set of rejected null hypotheses. As we did in the traditional algorithm, we initialize the counter of right-tail probability to 1 before performing the loop that approximates the null hypothesis distribution of the relationship statistic.

The permutation loop is now executed. Shuffle the target and initialize **max_f** to any number that is smaller than the smallest possible relationship statistic. This variable will keep track of the maximum relationship statistic in this replication. We now come to the part of the algorithm that distinguishes it from the traditional selection-bias algorithm. In that prior algorithm we found the maximum relationship statistic across all competing populations. But in this algorithm we exclude those competitors whose null hypotheses have already been rejected. So inside the loop that passes through all populations we process only those for which **passed** is FALSE. After we find the maximum we compare it to the original value of the competitor being tested and increment the right-tail probability counter if this null hypothesis value equals or exceeds the original value.

After all permutation replications are complete we have an estimate of the right-tail probability of the relationship statistic for competitor this_i. All we need to do at this point is compare this probability to the user-specified **alpha**. If it is is less than or equal to **alpha** we add it to the accumulated collection of passing competitors (those that we conclude have a relationship with the target). But if it did not pass we are done, so break out of the accumulation loop.

Here is a rough overview of my intuition for why this algorithm has an FWE of **alpha** with strong control, and also maximizes the average probability of rejecting false null hypotheses. My hope is that someone will make this more rigorous. I could have done this myself 40 years ago when I had my freshly minted statistics PhD, and I might still be able to do it, but at this point in my life I have too many other interests to devote significant time to this task.

Consider the best competitor, the one having the greatest relationship statistic and hence the one that we test first. Suppose its null hypothesis is true. By implication its relationship statistic will have the same distribution as that for all permutations (under the usual assumption that the target values are independent and identically distributed). Thus we will erroneously reject this null hypothesis with probability alpha. If we do so, it does not matter what errors we may subsequently make for other populations, because the definition of FWE is the probability that we will make one *or more* rejection errors. On the other hand, if we do not reject this null hypothesis, we are finished testing populations, so there is no more opportunity to make an error.

Now suppose the first null hypothesis is false. I claim that the permutation test as described is asymptotically the most powerful possible test for detecting this false null hypothesis. This should be a no-brainer, because we are testing the observed statistic against an asymptotically exact estimate of its actual distribution. If we declare this null hypothesis true (incorrectly, but not affecting FWE), we are finished testing populations for inclusion, so there is no more opportunity to make an error. If we declare it to be false we are correct and we advance to the next candidate.

When we advance to the next candidate, we are in exactly the same situation we were in with the first candidate, but now that first candidate is entirely removed from further computation. Its relationship statistic is no longer referenced, and that population no longer takes part in estimating the null hypothesis distribution of this next candidate. So if this second candidate's null hypothesis is true, we have probability alpha of incorrectly rejecting it. All other logic is exactly as it was for the first candidate.

This repeats until eventually we do not reject a null hypothesis, at which point we stop. We have alpha probability of having erroneously rejected a true null hypothesis at least once along the way, and thus we have a FWE of alpha, as desired. This fact holds regardless of how many null hypotheses are true, so thus our FWE has strong control, as desired. Finally, each time we encounter a false null hypothesis we employ the asymptotically most powerful test possible to test that hypothesis, and so we have maximum average probability of correctly rejecting false null hypotheses (asymptotically).

These assertions are distressingly heuristic, with little or nothing in the way of rigor to back them up. For my power arguments, I conveniently downplayed the fact that the null hypothesis distributions of the test statistics are only *asymptotically* correct, relying on the fact that if a great number of replications are used, the approximation is excellent. However, the intuition seems sound to me. Moreover, I have run massive quantities of Monte-Carlo simulations, using multiple alpha levels, multiple numbers of cases, multiple numbers of candidate populations, and various proportions of the candidates (from 0 to most) having false null hypotheses. In every case, the FWE came in at almost exactly the specified alpha level, well within normal variation tolerances. And this test has amazing power to detect even minuscule degrees of relationship between candidates and Y. So I am confident enough in its practical utility to use it in my own work and recommend it to others.

Demonstrating the Stepwise Algorithm

On Page 88 we saw a demonstration of indicator selection by optimal profit factor, using the traditional Monte-Carlo permutation test. Please keep handy the table of final results from that test. We now run exactly the same test, except using the new stepwise algorithm just described and with alpha=0.1. Here are those results:

```
Variable   profit factor   unbiased pval
  CMMA_10       1.597           0.005
   RSI_5        1.544           0.019
  RSI_10        1.475           0.078
  RTVY_6        1.462           0.098
```

```
Best remaining p-value=0.1960, so quitting
```

For the best two indicators the p-values are almost the same in both tests. (Theoretically, the first should be the same, because the two versions of the test are identical for the best performer. But these tests use random numbers, so small variation is likely. This is why it's important to use a large number of MCPT replications.) By the third, the p-value has dropped from 0.099 for the traditional test (which is an upper bound for the true value) to the true value of 0.078. For the fourth it drops from 0.123 to 0.098. This makes it just under my specified alpha of 0.1 so we pick up one more indicator at this alpha level, a clear demonstration of the increased power of the stepwise version. The fifth p-value, 0.1960, blows far past my alpha, so inclusion ceases.

It is tempting to use a larger alpha in order to see more computed p-values, but there is a serious potential problem with this if you are not careful. ***You must stop considering candidates as soon as the p-value passes your preset alpha.*** This is because raw p-values may actually decrease later. The Romano-Wolf reference cited at the beginning of this section solves this problem by forcing each successive p-value to be at least equal to the prior p-value, and they explain why this is necessary if p-values beyond that for the best competitor are to be used as actual p-values. I do the same in the code presented later. The explanation is far too complex for this text, so please see that paper for details.

Note that these p-values are computed using random numbers, so if you do not perform a large number of replications (thousands) you may occasionally find that the stepwise test produces a p-value slightly greater than that of the traditional test, which in theory should never happen. This is just random variation, easily fixed by using more replications.

Accelerating the Stepwise Algorithm

The algorithm shown on Page 94 is the best way to present the new stepwise algorithm, because it is a straightforward implementation of the mathematical statement. However, it is unnecessarily slow. This is because the block of permutations does not need to be repeated each time a new competitor is tested for inclusion (null hypothesis rejection). We need to do the set of m permutations only once, estimating all null hypothesis distributions simultaneously. Then we can do the stepwise inclusion after the permutations are complete.

To collect all distributions at once, we work from worst to best, updating the 'maximum so far' as each increasingly good competitor is added to the mix. Here is the fast but mathematically identical algorithm:

```
For i from 0 through n-1
   sort_indices[i] = i ;
   original[i] = relationship of competitor i with Y
   work[i] = original[i] ;

Sort work ascending, moving sort_indices simultaneously

-> Step 1 of 2: do the random replications and count right tail

For i from 0 through n-1
   count[i] = 1 ;                    Counts right-tail probability

For irep from 1 through m
   Shuffle Y

   max_f = number smaller than smallest possible relationship
   For i from 0 through n-1      Work from worst to best
     this_i = sort_indices[i]
     this_f = relationship between this_i and Y
     if (this_f > max_f)           Keep track of maximum
       max_f = this_f

   If (max_f >= original[this_i])
       ++count[this_i] ;           Count right-tail probability
     } // For irep

-> Step 2 of 2: Do the stepwise inclusion

   For i from n-1 through 0      Work from best to worst
     this_i = sort_indices[i]      Index of best remaining competitor
     If count[this_i] / (m+1) <= alpha
       Accept this competitor
     Else
       Break out of step loop; we are done
```

The slowest part of the selection-bias test is shuffling, whose time is proportional to the typically large number of cases. By computing all null hypothesis distributions in one replication loop we avoid a new set of shuffles every time we test a new candidate.

Code For the Fast Stepwise Algorithm

We now illustrate the algorithm shown on the prior page. This code is extracted from IND_FAM.CPP, a program that is identical to the IND.CPP program discussed on Page 81 except for two differences:

1) We use the new algorithm, so in addition to the prior parameters the user must also specify alpha, the maximum familywise error rate.

2) To simplify the code to be more understandable to the reader, only the maximum of the long and short profit factors is used as the performance criterion. The IND program also tested the long and short performance separately.

The program is called with five parameters as shown below. Please refer to the IND documentation on Page 81 for details.

```
IND_FAM   Floor   Alpha   Nreps   DataFile   ControlFile
```

We'll skip the code that's identical in both programs, or mundane. Assume that we have already computed the vector of original_crits. We have to sort them ascending and also keep track of the indices that point to the indicator at each performance rank. Then initialize the counters that keep track of the right-tail probabilities.

```
for (i=0 ; i<n_indicators ; i++) {
   sort_indices[i] = i ;
   dwork1[i] = original_crits[i] ;
   }
qsortdsi ( 0 , n_indicators-1 , dwork1 , sort_indices ) ; // Sort ascending

for (ivar=0 ; ivar<n_indicators ; ivar++)
   count[ivar] = 1 ;
```

We're now ready for the first of the two steps: the permutations that compute all null hypothesis distributions simultaneously. Here is this code, and a discussion follows.

```
for (irep=0 ; irep<nreps-1 ; irep++) {

  // Shuffle target
  i = ncases ;          // Number remaining to be shuffled
  while (i > 1) {        // While at least 2 left to shuffle
    j = (int) (unifrand() * i) ;
    if (j >= I)          // Cheap insurance against disaster if unifrand() returns 1.0
      j = i - 1 ;
    dummy = target_work[--i] ;
    target_work[i] = target_work[j] ;
    target_work[j] = dummy ;
    }

  // This loop processes competitors in order from poorest to best
  best_crit = -1.e60 ;
  for (ivar=0 ; ivar<n_indicators ; ivar++) {
    k = ind_index[sort_indices[ivar]] ;    // Column of ivar'th poorest in database
    for (i=0 ; i<ncases ; i++)
      ind_work[i] = data[i*nvars+k] ;       // Fetch it from database
    rho = spearman ( ncases , ind_work , target_work , dwork1 , dwork2 ) ;
    if (rho < 0.0) {  // Make sure that indicator and target are positively correlated
      for (i=0 ; i<ncases ; I++)           // Flip sign of this indicator
        ind_work[i] = -ind_work[i] ;
      }
    opt_thresh ( ncases , (int) (floor * ncases + 0.5) , 0 , ind_work , target_work ,
            &dummy , &dummy , &long_pf , &dummy , &short_pf , dwork1 , dwork2 ) ;
    best_pf = (long_pf > short_pf) ? long_pf : short_pf ; // Performance criterion

    if (best_pf > best_crit)
      best_crit = best_pf ;

    k = sort_indices[ivar] ;    // Index of ivar'th poorest indicator
    if (best_crit >= original_crits[k])
      ++count[k] ;
    } // For ivar, poorest to best
  } // For irep
```

It would be good to examine this code in conjunction with the algorithm shown on Page 99. The first step is to shuffle the target variable, bar-by-bar return in this application. The variable called *max_f* in the general algorithm is called best_crit in this specific application. We initialize it to a number vastly smaller than the smallest possible profit factor.

Then we work through all competing indicators, starting with the worst (smallest profit factor criterion) and progressing toward the best. Fetch into ind_work this indicator. Compute its nonparametric correlation with the target and flip its sign if the correlation is negative. Then find the optimal long and short profit factors and define our performance criterion as whichever is larger. As each new indicator enters the mix, update the maximum, best_crit. Finally, compare the current maximum to the original criterion for the current indicator. Update the right-tail count if indicated.

After all replications are complete we can perform the second of the two steps, adding indicators (rejecting null hypotheses) as long as we are able to avoid exceeding the user-specified alpha. In this case we work from the best to the worst, going backwards through sort_indices. For each, the p-value is the right-tail count divided by the total number of replications, including the original, with monotonicity enforced. As long as alpha is not exceeded we keep going, but as soon as it is exceeded we have to stop.

```
prior = 0.0 ;
fprintf ( fp_log , "\n\nBest of long/short profit factors and p-values..." ) ;
for (i=n_indicators-1 ; i>=0 ; i--) {
   k = sort_indices[i] ;
   pval = (double) count[k] / (double) nreps ;
   if (pval < prior)      // Enforce monotonicity as explained in Romano-Wolf
      pval = prior ;      // cited at the beginning of this section
   prior = pval ;
   if (pval <= alpha) {
      fprintf ( fp_log , "\n%15s %10.3lf %12.3lf",
            names[ind_index[k]], original_crits[k], pval ) ;
      }
   else {
      fprintf ( fp_log, "\n\nBest remaining p-value=%.4lf, so quitting", pval ) ;
      break ;
      }
   } // For all competitors, working from best to worst
```

4

Bootstrapping Trading Systems

We saw a brief intuitive introduction to the bootstrap on Page 14. It would be a good idea to review it now, even though we will actually be using a somewhat different and much more sophisticated algorithm in this chapter.

Here is the idea behind the applications we will consider in this chapter. Your trading system produces returns that can be measured on a regular basis. As has been pointed out in other contexts, such as computing profit factor for optimizing parameters, these returns should be measured at the finest resolution possible, typically bars. You should never perform the tests of this chapter on net returns of extended trades. For example, suppose you have a day-bar system whose trades are typically in the market for several days. You should not use the net return of such trades in these algorithms. Rather, you should mark the trades to market every day and use these finer resolution returns. You should do the corresponding thing for intraday trading, marking multiple-bar trades to the market for each bar.

So now we have a fine-resolution set of out-of-sample returns from our trading system. (Working with returns from in-sample data would be pointless because they have been optimized and hence have optimistic training bias.) What can we do with them? In this chapter we will learn how to use them to estimate confidence intervals for several parameters of the distribution of returns from this trading system.

What is meant by that last sentence? Our trading system, in combination with the market(s) being traded, gives rise to returns that come from some distribution. We assume that the distribution that will provide returns in the future is substantially similar to the distribution that gave rise to our collection of OOS returns. We will use our sample of OOS returns to tell us something about the distribution that provided them.

The most commonly considered parameter of a distribution is its mean. We don't know the mean of the distribution that provides our returns, but it does exist (in all practical applications here). We can estimate that mean as the mean of our obtained returns, but that's not enough information to be truly useful. What we really want to know is how confident we can be in that estimate. So we will use a bootstrap to make a confidence statement about the unknown mean of the distribution. For example, we might be able to say that there is a 90 percent chance that the annualized mean daily return of our trading system is at least 8 percent. We might also be interested in a statement such as "There is only a 10 percent chance that the annualized mean daily return is greater than 12 percent".

In theory at least we could use a bootstrap to estimate confidence intervals for a great many parameters of interest. For example, we could make probability statements about the the ratio of the distribution's mean to its standard deviation, which is essentially a basic Sharpe ratio. However, it is an unfortunate fact that parameters involving ratios are notoriously poor candidates for bootstrapping, so I will not do this here. Interested readers can find a detailed examination of this topic in my book *Assessing and Improving Prediction and Classification*.

The Bias-Corrected-Accelerated Bootstrap

There are several prominent bootstrap algorithms, as well as some less prominent algorithms. For our purposes, the best is almost certainly the *bias-corrected-accelerated algorithm*, usually abbreviated BC_a. Unfortunately, the mathematics that underpin this algorithm are fierce, far beyond the scope of this text. If you are interested, an excellent discussion can be found in *An Introduction to the Bootstrap* by Efron and Tibshirani. But be warned that this discussion involves very advanced mathematics, and if you do not have a solid background in mathematical statistics you needn't bother seeking out that reference.

The BC_a algorithm requires several steps, which are now discussed in separate short sections. Here's some nomenclature first. Recall from the discussion on Page 14 that we will be drawing (with replacement) many *bootstrap samples* (B of them) from our set of OOS returns, each sample containing as many returns as are in our collection of OOS returns. The parameter (mean or whatever) estimate for the original sample is $\hat{\theta}$, and $\hat{\theta}^{\star b}$ is the parameter estimate for the b'th bootstrap sample. Also, $\Phi(z)$ is the normal cumulative distribution function (CDF), and $\Phi^{-1}(p)$ is its inverse. The #[] operation counts how many times the inequality in the brackets holds true.

Computing the Bias Correction

The bias correction, roughly stated, compensates for the fact that the parameter estimates from the bootstrap samples under- or over-estimate the true parameter. The simpler bootstrap algorithms assume that the parameter of each bootstrap sample is an unbiased estimate of the true parameter value. To perform this correction we count how many of the bootstrapped parameter estimates are less than the estimate for the original sample. The bias correction is the inverse normal CDF of the fraction of the bootstrap results that are less than the grand value. This is expressed in Equation (4.1).

$$\hat{z}_0 = \Phi^{-1}\left(\frac{\#[\hat{\theta}^{*b} < \hat{\theta}]}{B} \right) \tag{4.1}$$

Computing the Acceleration

Simple bootstrap algorithms assume (very roughly stated!) that the standard deviation of the parameter estimate is independent of the actual parameter value. This is not always the case, so we correct for this in two steps. The first step involves a procedure called a *jackknife*. Suppose our OOS sample contains n returns. Once for each of these returns i we temporarily remove that case i and compute the parameter using the remaining $n-1$ cases. Let $\hat{\theta}_{(i)}$ designate this jackknifed parameter value. Let $\hat{\theta}_{(.)}$ be the mean of these n jackknifed values, as shown in Equation (4.2). Then the acceleration correction is given by Equation (4.3).

$$\hat{\theta}_{(.)} = \frac{1}{n} \sum_{i=1}^{n} \hat{\theta}_{(i)} \tag{4.2}$$

$$\hat{a} = \frac{\sum_{i=1}^{n} \left(\hat{\theta}_{(.)} - \hat{\theta}_{(i)} \right)^3}{6 \left[\sum_{i=1}^{n} \left(\hat{\theta}_{(.)} - \hat{\theta}_{(i)} \right)^2 \right]^{3/2}} \tag{4.3}$$

Computing the Lower and Upper Bounds

In the introductory material at the beginning of this chapter, we stated that our goal will be to make probability statements about the true value of some parameter of the distribution that supplies our returns. For example, we might wish to be able to state something similar to, "There is a 90 percent chance that the annualized mean daily return is at least 8 percent".

The α *fractile* of a distribution is the value such that there is probability α that an observation from the distribution is less than or equal to this value. For example, the 0.5 fractile of a distribution is its median. A much simpler type of bootstrap algorithm lets us estimate any confidence bound α for the parameter by finding the α fractile of the set of B bootstrap parameters, which we have already called $\hat{\theta}^{\star b}$ for b from 1 to B. This is usually called the *percentile method*. For example, suppose we find the 0.1 fractile of the collection of B bootstrap parameter estimates. Then we say that there is a probability of 0.1 that the parameter of the distribution is less than or equal to whatever this value is, and of course there is a probability of 0.9 that the parameter is greater. (For continuous parameters we can, with little bad conscience, be sloppy about equality or strict inequality at the endpoints.)

This simple method requires only minor modification to incorporate corrections for bias and acceleration. All we do is modify our desired α as shown in Equation (4.4). Note that if the bias and acceleration corrections are both zero, α is not changed.

$$\alpha' = \Phi\left(\hat{z}_0 + \frac{\hat{z}_0 + \Phi^{-1}(\alpha)}{1 - \hat{a}(\hat{z}_0 + \Phi^{-1}(\alpha))} \right) \tag{4.4}$$

To summarize this final step, we sort the B values of $\hat{\theta}^{\star b}$ into ascending order. Suppose we want a lower bound for the parameter, with α'<0.5. Then we select element k (indexed 1 through B), where k = α' (B+1), truncated down to an integer if there is a fractional remainder. For an upper bound, α'>0.5, let k = (1–α') (B+1), truncated down to an integer if there is a fractional remainder. Element B+1–k is the upper confidence bound.

A Program For Bounding the Mean

We now explore a simple program that uses the BC_a algorithm to find lower and upper confidence bounds for the mean daily (or whatever resolution is used) return. The BOOTMEAN directory contains the following files:

BOOTMEAN.CPP - The main program for performing the task
BOOT_CONF.CPP - the BC_a algorithm
RAND.CPP - Random number generator
QSORTD.CPP - Sorting algorithms
STATS.CPP - Basic statistical routines; used for normal CDF

The program is called with five parameters:

```
BOOTMEAN   Ntrain   Nboot   LowConf   HighConf   MarketFile
```

The *Ntrain* parameter specifies how many prices at the beginning of the market history are used to train the trading system. The remaining prices constitute the OOS test period that will supply the returns for the bootstrap test. The *Nboot* parameter specifies how many bootstrap samples are to be processed, and it would typically be 1,000 to 10,000, with more being better. The *LowConf* and *HighConf* parameters are the probabilities that the mean is below the corresponding computed bounds. Thus, *LowConf* should always be less than 0.5, and *HighConf* should always be greater than 0.5. Values of 0.1 and 0.9, respectively, are often reasonable.

The *MarketFile* parameter specifies the market history file, each of whose lines specifies the date as YYYYMMDD, the open, high, low, and close. Anything after these prices, such as volume, is ignored. Spaces, tabs, or commas may be used as delimiters. Here are two sample lines from a market history file:

```
19880211 122.32 122.89 121.42 121.92 4015
19880212 121.92 123.37 121.82 122.72 3544
```

The trading system used in this example program is the same trivial moving-average-crossover system used in the OVERFIT example; see the discussion on Page 49 for a review if needed. I won't waste space by showing it again here, although I will note that this implementation includes a subroutine that executes the trained trading system across a specified range of market history and computes the array of returns. The calling parameters for this system execution routine are as follows:

```
double execute (       // Returns profit factor
  int nprices ,        // Number of log prices in 'prices'
  int istart ,         // First trade decision is made on this price index
  double *prices ,     // Log prices
  int short_term ,     // Short-term lookback
  int long_term ,      // Long-term lookback
  int *nret ,          // Returns number of returns
  double *returns      // Returns returns
  )
```

This routine would typically be called with the entire price history supplied. The istart parameter would be the index of the last price in the training set, so that the return to the next price is the first OOS price. The optimal lookbacks found by the training routine are supplied, and it returns the number of OOS returns and the array of them.

If I had my way, the computed returns would just be the difference in log prices, a very sensible approach. However, most of the finance community prefers talking about percent or fractional returns relative to actual prices, so I compute the returns this way, under the assumption that the caller has supplied logs of actual prices. This is the line of code that does this:

```
returns[n++] = (exp(prices[i+1]) - exp(prices[i])) / exp(prices[i]) ; // Fractional return
```

When the main program prints the computed bounds, they are multiplied by 100 * 252 before printing. The 100 converts the fractional returns to percent, and the 252 (trading days in a year) annualizes the returns, assuming day bars.

After reading the market history, the code shown on the next page appears. The opt_params() routine was first presented on Page 49; please review that section if needed. To modify this program for your own trading system, all you need to change are opt_params() and execute().

```
opt_return = opt_params ( ntrain , close , &opt_short , &opt_long ) ; // Train

// Print the in-sample profit factor and optimal lookbacks here

opt_return = execute( nprices , ntrain-1 , close , opt_short , opt_long , &nret , returns );

// Print the OOS profit factor here

boot_conf_BCa ( nret , returns , param_mean , nboot , low_conf , high_conf ,
                 &low_bound , &high_bound , xwork , work2 ) ;

printf ( "\nUser-specified confidence limits = %.4lf %.4lf", low_conf , high_conf ) ;
printf ( "\nAnnualized daily percent confidence bounds = %.4lf %.4lf",
        100 * 252 * low_bound, 100 * 252 * high_bound ) ;
```

There are just three essential lines of code above. The call to opt_params() finds the long-term and short-term lookbacks that maximize the profit factor within the first ntrain prices in the market history. The call to execute() executes the optimized trading system on OOS data and returns the nret fractional returns in returns. Finally, boot_conf_BCa() performs the bootstrap computation of the confidence bounds. When the computed bounds are printed they are converted from fractional to annualized (assuming day bars) percent returns.

The boot_conf_BCa() routine must be given a subroutine that computes the parameter being bounded. In this program the parameter is the mean, so this subroutine is trivial:

```
double param_mean ( // Returns mean return
   int n ,                // Number of returns
   double *returns    // Log prices
   )
{
   int i ;
   double sum ;

   sum = 0.0 ;
   for (i=0 ; i<n ; i++)
     sum += returns[i] ;
   return sum / n ;
}
```

Code For the BCa Algorithm

We now present the boot_conf_BCa() routine. You will frequently need to turn back to its mathematical foundation which begins on Page 105. The calling parameter list is as follows:

```
void boot_conf_BCa (
   int n ,                    // Number of cases in sample
   double *x ,                // Variable in sample
   double (*user_t) (int , double * ) , // Compute parameter
   int nboot ,                // Number of bootstrap replications
   double low_conf ,          // Probability (<=0.5) of being below
   double high_conf ,         // Probability (>=0.5) of being below
   double *low_bound ,        // Output of lower 5% bound
   double *high_bound ,       // Output of upper 5% bound
   double *xwork ,            // Work area n long
   double *work2              // Work area nboot long
   )
```

The observations sampled from the population are supplied in x, and there are n of them. In our application, these are the OOS fractional returns. The caller supplies a subroutine user_t() that computes the parameter being bounded, which is just the mean here. The caller specifies the number of bootstrap replications and the desired low and high probabilities. This routine returns the low and high confidence bounds. It needs two work areas.

The first step is to compute the parameter for the original dataset, saving it in theta_hat. We also initialize the counter z0_count that will count the bias-correction terms in Equation (4.1).

```
int i, rep, k, z0_count ;
double param, theta_hat, theta_dot, z0, zlo, zhi, alo, ahi ;
double xtemp, xlast, diff, numer, denom, accel ;

theta_hat = user_t ( n , x ) ;      // Parameter for full set

z0_count = 0 ;                       // Will count for computing z0 later
```

The first loop computes and saves the parameter values for every bootstrap replication. While doing so it also cumulates z0_count as expressed in Equation (4.1).

```
for (rep=0 ; rep<nboot ; rep++) {   // Do all bootstrap reps (b from 1 to B)

   for (i=0 ; i<n ; i++) {          // Generate the bootstrap sample
      k = (int) (unifrand() * n) ;  // Select a case from the sample
      if (k >= n)                   // Should never happen, but be prepared
        k = n - 1 ;
      xwork[i] = x[k] ;             // Put bootstrap sample in xwork
      }

   param = user_t ( n , xwork ) ;   // Param for this bootstrap rep
   work2[rep] = param ;             // Save it for CDF later
   if (param < theta_hat)           // Count how many < full set param
     ++z0_count ;                   // For computing z0 later
   }
```

We complete Equation (4.1). Note that we must take precautions against the extremely unlikely but disastrous possibility that the count is at either extreme, in which case the inverse normal CDF would be undefined.

```
if (z0_count >= nboot)             // Prevent nastiness
   z0_count = nboot - 1 ;
if (z0_count <= 0)
   z0_count = 1 ;
z0 = inverse_normal_cdf ( (double) z0_count / (double) nboot ) ;
```

Now we perform the jackknife for computing the acceleration.

```
xlast = x[n-1] ;
theta_dot = 0.0 ;                  // For summing Equation (4.2)
for (i=0 ; i<n ; i++) {            // Jackknife
   xtemp = x[i] ;                  // Preserve case being temporarily removed
   x[i] = xlast ;                  // Swap in last case
   param = user_t ( n-1 , x ) ;    // Param for this jackknife
   theta_dot += param ;            // Cumulate mean across jackknife; Equation (4.2)
   xwork[i] = param ;              // Save for computing accel later
   x[i] = xtemp ;                  // Restore original case
   }
```

Compute the acceleration using Equation (4.3).

```
theta_dot /= n ;
numer = denom = 0.0 ;
for (i=0 ; i<n ; i++) {
   diff = theta_dot - xwork[i] ;
   xtemp = diff * diff ;
   denom += xtemp ;
   numer += xtemp * diff ;
   }

denom = sqrt ( denom ) ;
denom = denom * denom * denom ;
accel = numer / (6.0 * denom + 1.e-60) ;
```

The user-supplied confidence probabilities low_conf and high_conf are modified to alo and ahi using Equation (4.4).

```
zlo = inverse_normal_cdf ( low_conf ) ;
zhi = inverse_normal_cdf ( high_conf ) ;
alo = normal_cdf ( z0 + (z0 + zlo) / (1.0 - accel * (z0 + zlo)) ) ;
ahi = normal_cdf ( z0 + (z0 + zhi) / (1.0 - accel * (z0 + zhi)) ) ;
```

Finally, the saved bootstrapped parameters are sorted ascending and the correct terms are selected as described in the text at the end of the prior section.

```
qsortd ( 0 , nboot-1 , work2 ) ;       // Sort ascending

k = (int) (alo * (nboot + 1)) - 1 ;    // Unbiased fractile estimator
if (k < 0)
   k = 0 ;
*low_bound = work2[k] ;

k = (int) ((1.0-ahi) * (nboot + 1)) - 1 ;
if (k < 0)
   k = 0 ;
*high_bound = work2[nboot-1-k] ;
}
```

The Program In Action

I ran the BOOTMEAN program on OEX from early 1988 through the end
of 2019. To demonstrate the danger of using too short of an OOS period I
reserved just the final 100 days for OOS testing. This time period contains
almost uninterrupted upward movement, so the moving-average-
crossover system used by this program, being a powerful trend follower,
performs extremely well. To obtain honest results, the OOS time period
should encompass a wide variety of market conditions. The output from
this program is as follows:

```
8036 prices were read.  Training with the first 7936...
Profit factor based on log prices = 1.09006
optimal long lookback = 243  short lookback = 17
OOS profit factor = 1.46707 with 100 returns
User-specified confidence limits = 0.1000 0.5000
Annualized daily percent confidence bounds = 1.1811 26.9889
```

Notice that the in-sample profit factor is a meager 1.09, and this was
obtained by optimizing the lookbacks! Clearly this is a pretty poor trading
system. But the OOS profit factor is a very respectable 1.467. We also see
that there is a 10 percent probability (0.1) that the mean annualized daily
percent return is 1.18 or less, nothing to write home about. On the other
hand, there is a 50 percent chance (0.5) that the mean annualized daily
percent return could exceed 26.99!

Yikes, why is the range so wide? The reason is simply that I used just 100
days in the OOS period. That's not enough cases to get decent confidence
bounds from any statistical procedure. Splitting the market history in half
gives very different results. Especially noteworthy is the fact that although
the OOS profit factor drops to a measly 1.03, the lower bound actually
increases to 1.6! This is a direct result of having many more OOS returns
on which to base the computation.

```
8036 prices were read.  Training with the first 4036...
Profit factor based on log prices = 1.14107
optimal long lookback = 219  short lookback = 5
OOS profit factor = 1.03370 with 4000 returns
User-specified confidence limits = 0.1000 0.5000
Annualized daily percent confidence bounds = 1.6286 7.4003
```

Probability of Significant Drawdowns

Drawdowns haunt the sleep of market traders. It is inevitable that investment equity will bounce up and down. But how far down might it drop from its peak? There are at least three questions related to drawdown that concern traders:

- We have just developed a candidate trading system but not yet put it to work. Is the level of drawdown that we can expect to see *regularly* acceptable to us, or should we reject our candidate trading system and search for one with less drawdown expected?

- How likely is it that our candidate system could experience a truly catastrophic drawdown?

- We are trading our system. Is the drawdown that we are currently experiencing consistent with what we determined was expected when we developed the system, or has something perhaps gone very wrong and we should stop trading immediately?

In this section I will present a program that trains a trading system (you can easily substitute your own trading system in the code), executes the system on out-of-sample data, and then computes and prints percent drawdowns that could be expected with user-specified probabilities. This program can be used to answer all three questions above, although the developer must be aware that *these computations are all approximations and are subject to significant, unavoidable random error.*

Defining Drawdown

I have encountered several different definitions of drawdown in my years of consulting for financial institutions, so it is crucial that I rigorously define drawdown as I compute it in this section, lest there be misunderstandings. I strongly believe that my definition is the most appropriate, but if you disagree it is easy to modify my drawdown routine to implement your own definition.

I compute drawdown by assuming that as the current equity of a trading system rises and falls, this current equity is continuously reinvested in the system. This would obviously be the case for a single trade that is marked to market regularly. But it also applies to getting out of the market and then back in. For example, suppose we initially invest $1000 in our trading system. Our equity rises to $1200 and then falls to $1100, at which point we decide to exit the market. Later, when we reenter the market we do so with an equity of $1100.

Suppose our equity then drops to $900 before recovering. Our drawdown experienced during this time period is the peak-to-trough drop in equity expressed as a percentage of the peak equity. In this case, the drawdown would be 100 * (1200 – 900) / 1200 = 25 percent.

Because I always prefer working with logs of prices and equity, I take a different route to get to the same result. The drawdown in the log domain is DD_{log} = log(1200) – log(900) = log(1200/900) = 0.2877. Equation (4.5) shows how to convert this to a percent drop. In this example, we get a percent drawdown of 100 * [1–exp(-.2877)] = 100 * [1–0.75] = 25 percent. I leave it as an exercise for the reader to verify the correctness of Equation (4.5). Begin by pondering the meaning of the exponentiated term.

$$DD_{pct} = 100 * \left[1 - \exp\left(-DD_{log}\right)\right] \qquad (4.5)$$

Note that this process assumes we are in a situation in which it is impossible to lose more than we have invested, which would be the case when purchasing equities, bonds, and so forth. If, on the other hand, we are purchasing futures contracts or shorting instruments, we would normally stay in the original price domain rather than taking logs. In such a situation we would also generally need to assume a starting equity. The code shown throughout the remainder of this section can handle this situation with minimal revision. The drawdown() routine shown on the next page would be called with absolute equity changes rather than logs, and the cumulative and maximum equity would be initialized to the desired starting equity instead of zero. Finally, the loss would be computed as a percent of the maximum. Other code would remain unchanged.

Code for Drawdown

The code shown below computes maximum absolute drawdown, which is what we want when the trade returns are the log of the equity change (ratio of new to prior) produced by the trade. When drawdown is reported to the user later, Equation (4.5) can be used to convert the log-domain drawdown to the more familiar percent-of-peak.

```
double drawdown (
  int n ,            // Number of trades
  double *trades   // They are here, usually log of equity change ratio
  )
{
  int icase ;
  double cumulative, max_equity, loss, dd ;

  cumulative = max_equity = dd = 0.0 ;

  for (icase=0 ; icase<n ; icase++) {
    cumulative += trades[icase] ;          // Cumulative log equity
    if (cumulative > max_equity)           // Keep track of peak
      max_equity = cumulative ;
    else {                                 // We are in a drawdown period
      loss = max_equity - cumulative ;
      if (loss > dd)                       // Keep track of max drawdown
        dd = loss ;
      }
    } // For all cases

  return dd ;
}
```

We initialize the cumulative equity, its peak value, and the maximum drawdown to zero. Then we pass through the trades, cumulating the net equity as we go. If the cumulative equity exceeds the peak so far, update the peak to this new value. But if we have dropped below the peak we are in a drawdown period. Compare the drop from the peak to the maximum drop so far (**dd**), and if we set a new record, update it. When done we return that maximum drawdown.

Drawdown Percentiles as Parameters

We often talk about some *parameter* of a distribution. In the context of this chapter, the distribution in which we are interested is the hypothetical collection of possible trade returns. There is some theoretical distribution from which trade returns are drawn. We already drew some returns when we executed our trading system on out-of-sample data and marked the returns to market at the finest possible resolution. If we put our trading system to work with real money we will draw more returns from this same (we certainly hope!) distribution. So we can talk about parameters of this distribution of returns.

The most commonly discussed parameter of a distribution is its mean. We studied bootstrap tests involving the mean at the beginning of this chapter. Now we will consider a much more complex parameter of the distribution of returns.

Suppose we consider a specified number of returns arranged in sequence. (Since the returns are random and presumed independent, randomly sequencing them is legitimate.) We can compute the drawdown associated with this set of ordered returns. The hypothetical set of such drawdowns is itself a distribution and hence we can talk about parameters of this distribution. In particular, we can talk about percentiles of this distribution of drawdowns. The 50th percentile is the median, which may be of some interest, since by definition there is a 50-50 chance that our drawdown will exceed this amount. Of greater interest would be large percentiles, such as the 90th or even the 99th. If we were to know, say, the 90th percentile of the distribution of drawdowns, we would by definition know that only 10 percent of the time would we expect the drawdown to exceed this value. If, for example, we found that the 90th percentile were, say, 4.5 percent, we would be ecstatic, at least as far as drawdown goes. On the other hand, if we found that the 50th percentile were 57 percent we would toss that trading system in the trash.

Do note that a key part of defining this parameter, a percentile of the distribution of drawdowns, is our specified number of returns in the time period over which the drawdown is measured. If there are more returns, there will be greater potential for large drawdowns.

Unfortunately, to quote the great modern philosopher Mick Jagger, "You can't always get what you want." At the beginning of this chapter, when we considered the mean return, we observed that it was impossible to know the true mean of the distribution of returns. We could compute the mean of the out-of-sample returns and assume that it was probably somewhat close to the population mean. More rigorously, we could apply a bootstrap test to the OOS returns and thereby make some probability statements about the true population mean.

The same applies to the parameter currently under discussion, a specified percentile of the distribution of drawdowns measured over a specified time period. We can use the subroutine shown soon to approximate the desired percentile of drawdowns *produced by the sample of OOS returns*. But this is not equal to the true population parameter, because our sample of OOS returns is just a random sample, not an exhaustive representation of the entire population. So in order to achieve a more rigorous result we will perform a bootstrap test that allows us to make a probability statement about the true population parameter.

But first we need to see how to estimate the parameter from our OOS sample. I am not aware of any fast direct algorithm for accomplishing this task, and I strongly suspect that no such algorithm exists. So I reverted to brute-force Monte-Carlo simulation. For a large number of replications (at least a thousand or so, and preferably more), randomly select returns from the OOS set, as many as specified for the length of the drawdown test period. For each replication, compute the drawdown. Then sort the obtained drawdowns and find the desired percentile (or fractile in this code). The calling parameter list is as follows:

```
double drawdown_fractile ( // Fractile corresponding to dd_conf
  int n_returns ,        // Number of trade returns (available history)
  int n_trades ,         // Number of trades in drawdown period
  double *returns ,      // n_returns trade returns (available history)
  int n_reps ,           // Number of reps used to compute fractile
  double dd_conf ,       // Desired fractile 0-1
  double *trade_work ,   // Work area n_trades long
  double *work           // Work area n_reps long
  )
```

The first parameter is the number of returns in the OOS sample set, and the second parameter is the number of returns that will make up the time period over which drawdown is to be measured. These two quantities need not be equal, and in fact in many practical applications n_trades will be less, often much less, than n_returns.

As is my habit, returns will nearly always be the log ratios of equity changes, as discussed in the prior section on computing drawdown. The number of replications, n_reps, should be as large as is practical, certainly at least 1,000 or so, because this determines the accuracy with which the percentile is approximated. The desired fractile, dd_conf, is just the percentile divided by 100. We also need two work areas as shown.

The algorithm is straightforward. For each replication we randomly select, with replacement, n_trades returns and compute the drawdown. After we have n_reps drawdowns we sort them ascending and extract the element closest to the desired fractile.

```
{
  int i, k, irep ;

  for (irep=0 ; irep<n_reps ; irep++) {
    for (i=0 ; i<n_trades ; i++) {
      k = (int) (unifrand() * n_returns) ;
      if (k >= n_returns)     // Will never happen if unifrand() < 1
        k = n_returns - 1 ;
      trade_work[i] = returns[k] ;
      }
    work[irep] = drawdown ( n_trades , trade_work ) ;
    }

  qsortd ( 0 , n_reps-1 , work ) ;

  k = (int) (dd_conf * (n_reps+1) ) - 1 ;
  if (k < 0)
    k = 0 ;
  return work[k] ;
}
```

Recall from Page 110 that the boot_conf_BCa() routine must be given a subroutine that computes the parameter being bounded. This subroutine must have just two parameters, the number of observations (returns) and the array of their values. However, the drawdown_fractile() routine has many more parameters, including the length of the drawdown period, the desired fractile, the number of replications, and two work areas. I handle this by making these five extra parameters statics at the top of the program and then defining a simple wrapper routine that satisfies the requirements of the bootstrap routine but still passes all required parameters to the drawdown_fractile() routine.

```
static int ntrades ;      // Number of trades in drawdown period
static int nreps ;        // Number of reps for computing dd fractile
static double ddconf ;   // Desired fractile fraction 0-1
static double *work_ntrades ;
static double *work_nreps ;

double param_ddfrac ( int n_returns , double *returns )
{
   return drawdown_fractile ( n_returns , ntrades , returns , nreps , ddconf ,
                         work_ntrades , work_nreps ) ;
}
```

This is a good time to bring up a potentially sensitive topic. In my work as a consultant to the finance industry, I have occasionally run into situations in which a developer estimates drawdown probabilities by using only the algorithm in drawdown_fractile() or some algorithm that may be slightly more complex but ultimately similar in behavior. *This is equivalent to asserting that the true population mean of a set of returns is equal to the mean of the sampled OOS returns, and it is just as* **incorrect**.

The logic of this incorrect approach is deceptively simple: the returns are out-of-sample and hence an unbiased representation of the true population. All that will vary in the future are the returns (wins and losses) that appear, and the order in which they appear. If many times we randomly select returns from our OOS return set and compute the drawdowns, the distribution of these drawdowns will be representative of future drawdowns that we may experience. So if we compute a percentile of this distribution we can assume that this is the population percentile.

The fatal flaw in this algorithm is that it fails to account for the fact that the OOS set is itself a random sample and hence a source of variation that *must* be accounted for. And what makes this flaw especially bad is that the errors it introduces are the worst possible sort: this flawed algorithm *underestimates* the probability of drawdowns. This is especially true for catastrophic drawdowns, in which case it can easily underestimate the probability by a factor of ten or more. (See my book *Testing and Tuning Market Trading Systems* for a detailed discussion of this issue.) The correct approach is to use a bootstrap to make probability statements about the true drawdown percentile, rather than just asserting that the sample value equals the true population value.

The BOOTDD Program for Bounding Drawdowns

On Page 108 we explored the BOOTMEAN program that finds confidence bounds for the true population mean return based on an out-of-sample set of returns. Please review that section as needed, because the BOOTDD program of this section will use the same primitive trading system and create an OOS set in exactly the same way. However, the invocation of the BOOTDD program is somewhat more complex because there are special parameters involved.

The program is called with seven parameters:

```
BOOTDD  Ntrain  Ntrades  Nboot  Nreps  DDconf  BootConf
MarketFile
```

The *Ntrain* parameter specifies how many prices at the beginning of the market history are used to train the trading system. The remaining prices constitute the OOS test period that will supply the returns for the bootstrap test. The *Ntrades* parameter is the number of trades in the drawdown period. The *Nboot* parameter specifies how many bootstrap samples are to be processed, and it would typically be at least 1,000, with more being better. The *Nreps* parameter specifies how many replications are used to estimate the sample drawdown fractile, and it would typically be at least 1,000, with more being better. The *DDconf* parameter is the desired fractile for the drawdown, and it would typically be close to 1, probably in the range of 0.9 for uncommon but possible drawdowns, to 0.999 for almost impossibly rare but potentially catastrophic drawdowns. The *BootConf* parameter is the desired fractile for the bootstrapped lower bound, and it will generally be around 0.9 to 0.99 or so. These parameters are discussed in more detail on Page 125 when we experiment with the program.

The *MarketFile* parameter specifies the market history file, each of whose lines specifies the date as YYYYMMDD, the open, high, low, and close. Anything after these prices, such as volume, is ignored. Spaces, tabs, or commas may be used as delimiters. Here are two sample lines from a market history file:

```
19880211 122.32 122.89 121.42 121.92 4015
19880212 121.92 123.37 121.82 122.72 3544
```

The BOOTDD directory contains the following files:
    BOOTDD.CPP - The main program for performing the task
    BOOT_CONF.CPP - the BC_a algorithm
    RAND.CPP - Random number generator
    QSORTD.CPP - Sorting algorithms
    STATS.CPP - Basic statistical routines; used for normal CDF

The trading system used in this example program is the same trivial
moving-average-crossover system used in the OVERFIT and BOOTMEAN
examples; see the discussions on Pages 49 and 108 for a review if needed.
I won't waste space by showing it again here, although I will note that you
can easily substitute your own trading system by replacing the training
and execution routines.

We skip over the mundane task of reading the market history file, whose
code can be found in BOOTDD.CPP. As was done in the BOOTMEAN
program, the first step is to compute the optimal lookback parameters
using the user-specified number of training cases, and then execute the
system on the remaining history to get our out-of-sample set of returns:

```
opt_params ( ntrain , close , &opt_short , &opt_long ) ; // Train
execute ( nprices , ntrain-1 , close , opt_short , opt_long , &nret , returns ) ; // Get OOS
```

To demonstrate the *incorrect* way to estimate the drawdown fractile, we
simply call the parameter estimation routine:

```
dummy = param_ddfrac ( nret , returns ) ;  // Estimate drawdown fractile from OOS
dummy = 100.0 * (1.0 - exp ( -dummy )) ;   // Equation (4.5)
// Print this incorrect value here
```

Finally, we use the bootstrap to compute a probability-based bound for the
drawdown fractile. We can use either tail, as they will be practically equal.
I specify **boot_conf** for both tails and arbitrarily choose the left tail.

```
boot_conf_BCa ( nret , returns , param_ddfrac , nboot , boot_conf , boot_conf ,
                &bound , &dummy , xwork , work2 ) ;

dummy = 100.0 * (1.0 - exp ( -bound )) ;    // Equation (4.5)
// Print this bound here
```

Demonstrating the BOOTDD Program

We now execute the BOOTDD program with several sets of parameters. To make sure the meaning of the two specified probabilities (*DDconf* and *BootConf*) is clear, we'll review this topic first, even though it was already covered on Page 119. I freely admit that having *two* probabilities involved is confusing, not to mention annoying. Yet I assure you, this approach is necessary, unavoidable.

First, consider *DDconf*. If there were no such thing as random variation in our out-of-sample return set, this would be the only probability we would need. When we specify this probability, we are asking for the drawdown threshold that has the property that there is *DDconf* probability that future drawdowns will be less than or equal to the computed threshold. For example, suppose we specify *DDconf*=0.9, along with a drawdown period (such as a year of returns). Also, suppose that through some sort of magic the program were able to tell us that this threshold is a drawdown of 14.3 percent. This means that in any future drawdown period of the specified length, there is a 90 percent chance that the drawdown we will experience will not exceed 14.3 percent.

We can choose *DDconf* according to the frequency of drawdowns we are interested in. The 0.9 used above is often reasonable, because it provides a threshold for a degree of drawdown that will not happen often but that is nevertheless possible in real life. At first glance it might seem as though we would want to specify this probability very close to 1, perhaps 0.99999. But the problem is that when we ask for such an immense degree of certainty, we would most likely get a drawdown threshold that is so large that in practice it would be useless to us. We might, however, be interested in a much smaller *DDconf*, perhaps as small as 0.5. This will give us a 'median' drawdown, a value having the property that there is about equal probability that the drawdown we will actually experience will be greater than or less than this value.

If only things were as simple as what I just presented. Alas, the calculations that translate a specified *DDconf* into a drawdown threshold are not based on complete knowledge of the distribution of returns. Rather, these calculations are based on our OOS return set, which is nothing more than a random sample from the true population of returns. Therefore, a threshold computed from the OOS return set will not equal the true population threshold, which I will call the *DDconf threshold*.

Due to this unavoidable fact, we must specify a second probability, the *BootConf*. In practice this will always be large, typically 0.9 to 0.99 or so. This is the probability that the computed threshold equals or exceeds the true but unknown *DDconf threshold*.

For example, suppose we specify *DDconf*=0.95 and *BootConf*=0.9. This says that we are ultimately interested in the drawdown threshold which has the property that there is a 95 percent chance that our future drawdown will not exceed this threshold. Unfortunately, there is no way to compute this threshold. But what we can do is compute an upper bound for it. The program will give us a drawdown threshold that has a 90 percent chance of being greater than or equal to the true but unknown *DDconf threshold*. In other words, we can be 90 percent sure that the threshold that we really want but cannot compute does not exceed the threshold that we do find.

Okay, it's time for a few examples. In every case that follows we will be using OEX from early 1988 through the end of 2019. The moving-average-crossover lookbacks will be optimized using the first 7000 days of this dataset, and the remaining 1036 days served as the OOS return set. The drawdown period was 252 days, about a year of trading. There were 2000 bootstrap replications and also 2000 to estimate the fractile threshold. In the first test, *DDconf*=*BootConf*=0.9, a reasonable middle-of-the-road parameter set. The following results were obtained:

```
Profit factor based on log prices = 1.09197
    optimal long lookback = 218   short lookback = 32
OOS profit factor = 1.06580 with 1036 returns
Incorrectly computed confidence bound for drawdown = 16.6480
percent
BootConf bound for true DDconf drawdown = 21.1261 percent
```

As usual for primitive trading systems, the profit factors are not exciting, although the OOS profit factor does show some positive return. The important thing to note here is that the drawdown threshold correctly computed, 21.1, is significantly greater than the incorrectly computed value of 16.6.

Now let's bump *DDconf* up to 0.99 while leaving *BootConf* at 0.9. This gives us the following thresholds (everything else remains the same):

```
Incorrectly computed confidence bound for drawdown = 23.1036
percent
BootConf bound for true DDconf drawdown = 31.6871 percent
```

Notice how the drawdown thresholds jumped significantly. Of course, if we demand such a high probability for *DDconf* we probably also want to be very sure of ourselves on the quality of the computed bound. So let's set *DDconf=BootConf=0.99*. This give us the following:

```
Incorrectly computed confidence bound for drawdown = 23.1036
percent
BootConf bound for true DDconf drawdown = 34.8336 percent
```

Naturally, the incorrectly computed bound remains the same, because that computation neglects the vital bootstrap that compensates for the OOS return set being a random sample. But interestingly enough, bumping up *BootConf* from the fairly modest 0.9 to the much stricter 0.99 doesn't cost us a lot; the drawdown threshold increases from 31.7 to 34.8. But the gap between the incorrect and correct thresholds widens to an even more massive amount.

Finally, let's go for a real middle-of-the-road threshold, setting the parameters to *DDconf=BootConf=0.5*. This says that we ideally want a threshold such that there is equal probability that our achieved drawdown will be above or below this threshold, a median drawdown that we can expect. Moreover, we want to use the bootstrap to give us a threshold that has equal chance of being above or below the true threshold. The following output results:

```
Incorrectly computed confidence bound for drawdown = 9.7840
percent
BootConf bound for true DDconf drawdown = 10.1352 percent
```

Unsurprisingly, the drawdown thresholds are much smaller than we saw in the prior examples. It is also noteworthy, and not unexpected, that the correctly and incorrectly computed thresholds are about the same. This is because the randomness of our OOS sample has the greatest impact on extreme drawdowns, and not much on middling drawdowns.

5

Confirming Superiority

Trading system development is all about superiority; we study alternative approaches and choose the best as defined by some criterion that we believe to be appropriate. But is the 'best' truly the *BEST*? If there is a substantial probability that the winner could have obtained its exalted position by sheer luck rather than by truly outstanding performance then we should reconsider our choice. Assessing our degree of confidence in our selection is an important and often neglected aspect of trading system development. Consider the following situations:

- We task several employees, who have different ideas about market behavior, to present to management their best trading system. We choose the best performer, with the plan of promoting that person, or giving their trading system a privileged slot in the company portfolio.

- We have developed a trading system that performs satisfactorily in some market, perhaps a broad market index. Then we test it in a variety of other markets, perhaps an industrial index, and a financial index, and a transportation index, and so forth. Our plan is that we will ultimately trade the system mostly or only in whichever market provides the best performance.

- We have a vast collection of indicators that we screen for their relationship to future market behavior. One or a few stand out from the rest, so we decide to work strictly with the outstanding performers.

- We have developed some powerful indicator that, like nearly all indicators, requires that we specify a lookback, the number of recent historical prices that are examined in order to compute a value for the indicator. We want to choose the optimal lookback for our task.

- We have a trading system that tells us when to open a position in the market, but we don't have a good exit strategy. Perhaps signals from this trading system have an optimal holding period, and we should just hold our position for that predetermined length of time and then close the position. What is the optimal holding period?

One important aspect of testing for true superiority is that context is important. For example, suppose we include a vast quantity of worthless competitors along with one or a very few somewhat good competitors. Even if the 'good' one or ones are not very good at all, they will still be shown to be superior to their worthless competitors, a possibly misleading result. So whenever possible it is good to pre-test the competitors to confirm that they have some value. If this is not practical, then at least you should be careful to avoid including competitors that you have reasonable belief will not provide true competition.

The converse is also important: we want competition. For example, suppose we have a powerful indicator, and its ideal lookback is about 1000 bars. There would be little point in testing a competitor set consisting of lookbacks of 998, 999, 1000, 1001, and 1002 bars. These competitors would all perform so similarly that even if the performance of each were excellent, in all likelihood none would stand out from the others, and the 'truly best' test discussed in this chapter will report no true superiority. This would not be a disaster; after all, it's true! But what's the point? You've just wasted a bunch of computer and human time to get a worthless result.

The bottom line is that to get a superiority test that is unlikely to be either misleading or without value, you should make a reasonable effort to choose competitors that are both varied and individually likely to be good. You want neither excessive homogeneity nor a large quantity of worthless competitors. Always remember that this test is highly dependent on the set of competitors; it rates each competitor *relative to the competition*. It's primary role is not so much to test the *individual quality* of a competitor as to assess the likelihood that an apparently *superior* competitor achieved its superior position via true power versus good luck. It does so by seeing if good training-set performance carries over to a test set.

I should say that the original inspiration for the family of tests presented in this chapter came from a wonderful 2015 paper called "The Probability of Backtest Overfitting" by David H. Bailey et al. I have both modified their algoithm and extended it to a wider variety of applications. However, the credit for the marvelous idea unpinning this test belongs fully to those authors.

Overview of the Algorithm

Here is the general idea behind this superiority test. Suppose we were to randomly divide the dataset in half, designating one half to be a 'training' set and the other half a test set. Considering only the training set, determine which of the competitors has the best (in-sample) performance. I hesitate to use the word 'training' set because no parameters other than a trade threshold can be optimized; we'll speak more on this later. All we are allowed to do is compare performance of the competitors on half of the data. When this step is finished, we will have a performance measure for each competitor, and we will know which competitor has the best such performance.

Next, we compute the test-set performance of all competitors. Find the median test-set performance of all competitors. Compare this median to the test-set performance of the competitor that was best in the training set. If this best performer in the training set has truly outstanding capability, then this capability will carry through to the test set; its test-set performance will probably be superior to the median test-set performance of all competitors. On the other hand, if the best in-sample competitor achieved its position mostly by good luck rather than superiority, its test-set performance may be greater than or less than the median, randomly. Take note of whether the test-set performance of the best in-sample performer beat the median.

That's a single iteration, which is not enough for reliable results. Among other things, it provides just a single binary result: the best was or was not superior to the median. Moreover, the split into a training set and a test set may have been lucky or unlucky in some way. So we do another random train/test split and repeat the process just described. After doing this random split many times (hundreds or thousands) we have a count of how many times the competitor that was best in the training set failed to outperform the median of all competitors. True superiority will cause this count to be small. If we divide this count by the number of iterations, we have a probability that the 'best in training set' performer will fail to carry through to the test set, and we can treat this probability almost as if it were a traditional p-value (although really it's not; the resemblance is superficial).

A good way to conceptualize the algorithm is to visualize the data as laid out in a matrix. Each column corresponds to a different competitor, and each row corresponds to an observation. In our current context the observations will usually be log returns from a trading system, and the performance criterion for a column (competitor) will be something like profit factor computed down the rows. However, there are other possibilities. For example, the rows might be values of the indicator corresponding to a column and the performance criterion might be mutual information between that column and market returns or some other measure of future market movement. This is the approach taken in my *VarScreen* program, available for free download from my website, and this approach is discussed in detail in my book "Data Mining Algorithms in C++". Here we will work strictly with the observations being trading system returns. The chart below shows this layout for 6 observations from 3 competitors. Note that this is the layout used in the original Bailey et al paper, and I showed it this way for readers who want to refer back to that paper. In my code I structure it as the transpose of this layout for reasons of computational efficiency that will be obvious later.

Competitors

O	Obs 1 Comp 1	Obs 1 Comp 2	Obs 1 Comp 3	...
b				
s	Obs 2 Comp 1	Obs 2 Comp 2	Obs 2 Comp 3	...
e				
r	Obs 3 Comp 1	Obs 3 Comp 2	Obs 3 Comp 3	...
v				
a	Obs 4 Comp 1	Obs 4 Comp 2	Obs 4 Comp 3	...
t				
i	Obs 5 Comp 1	Obs 5 Comp 2	Obs 5 Comp 3	...
o				
n	Obs 6 Comp 1	Obs 6 Comp 2	Obs 6 Comp 3	...
s				

The training set is defined by randomly selecting half of the rows, and the test set is made up of the remaining rows. The easiest way to do this is to initialize an array of integers to index the rows and then shuffle this array. We simply declare that the indices in the first half of the shuffled array define the training set, and the others define the test set.

The general algorithm, shown below, is directly applicable to many or most applications of superiority testing, and very close for the rest. Explanations for these steps are given on the next page.

```
1)  | Compute the market returns as log(Next/Current)
    |
2)  | for icomp from 0 through n_competitors-1
3)  |     counts[icomp] = 0.0 ;
    |
4)  | for ibar from 0 through n_bars-2
5)  |     index[ibar] = ibar ;
    |
6)  | for irep from 0 through n_reps-1
7)  |     Shuffle index
    |
8)  |     for icomp from 0 through n_competitors-1  (Training phase)
9)  |         sort_key[icomp] = icomp ;
10) |         Optionally optimize trading threshold for this competitor
11) |         criters[icomp] = training-set criterion for icomp
12) |     Sort criters ascending, simultaneously moving sort_keys
    |
13) |     for icomp from 0 through n_competitors-1  (Test phase)
14) |         criters[icomp] = test-set criterion for icomp
15) |     median = Median ( criters[0], ..., criters[n_competitors-1] )
    |
16) |     for icomp from 0 through n_competitors-1  (Counting phase)
17) |         if (criters[sort_key[icomp]] <= median)
18) |             ++counts[icomp] ;
    |
19) | for icomp from 0 through n_competitors-1
20) |     counts[icomp] /= nreps
    |
21) | for icomp from 0 through n_competitors-1  (Presentation phase)
22) |     sort_key[icomp] = icomp ;
23) |     Optionally optimize trading threshold for this competitor
24) |     criters[icomp] = entire dataset criterion for icomp
25) | Sort criters ascending, simultaneously moving sort_keys
    |
26) | for icomp from n_competitors-1 through 0 (decrementing)
27) |     print name[sort_key[icomp]], criters[icomp], counts[icomp]
```

First we pass through the market history and compute returns, typically as the log ratio of the next bar's close to the current bar's close. Other variations are possible. A more sophisticated approach would be to compute the return as the log change from the next bar's open to the open two bars from now, thus avoiding the implicit assumption that you are able to open a trade at the close of a bar. You may scale returns by a measure of volatility such as average true range. If the competitors are different markets you will need a separate return vector for each market.

The vector **counts** will sum for each competitor the count across replications of the number of times that competitor's test-set performance failed to exceed the median performance. It will later be converted to a probability vector, so it should be a real, not an integer. Zero it.

The vector **index** indexes cases for distinguishing those in the training set from those in the test set. If there are **n_bars** bars of price history, we will have only **n_bars–1** returns because we are looking ahead one bar into the future to find returns. Initialize this vector to an identity.

We now begin the replication loop. The first step is to shuffle the **index** vector. In all of the code that will appear later we will let the first half of this vector be the indices of the training-set cases, with the second half identifying the test-set cases.

Lines 8 through 12 handle the training phase of a replication. We initialize **sort_key** to be an identity vector; we'll see why soon. For each competitor, if we need to optimize a threshold (or perhaps two, for long/short systems) we do so here. This is discussed in the next section. Then we pass through the training set, cumulating a performance criterion. In my own work, this usually involves computing the profit factor based on market returns that correspond to a competitor's indicator value exceeding a threshold.

Line 12 lets us rank competitors based on their training-set performance. We sort **criters** ascending, and whatever swaps are done to attain this are duplicated in **sort_keys**. Thus, after this operation, **sort_keys[0]** will be the index of the competitor that had the worst performance, **sort_keys[1]** will be the index of the second worst performer, and so forth, with **sort_keys[n_competitors-1]** identifying the best performer.

Lines 13-15 handle the test-set computations. If we optimized thresholds in line 10 above we must use these same thresholds when processing the test set. We compute the test-set performance of each competitor and then find the median of these values.

Lines 16-18 are potentially confusing, so please be sure that you understand them before moving on. If we were comparing criters[icomp] to the median, then counts[icomp] would refer to competitor icomp. But we don't care about counting any individual competitor at this point. Recall that our primary goal, the original motivation for this whole algorithm, is to count failures for the *best* competitor, and this probably will change from replication to replication. (As will be seen, we can generalize beyond just the best. More on this subject later.) Thus, we compare criters[sort_key[icomp]] to the median. In other words, the comparison is not to a specific competitor, but rather to a *rank*. When we do it this way, we will have counts[n_competitors–1] being our main object of interest, the number of failures of the *best* training-set performer, regardless of which competitor this happens to be on a given replication. Counts for other ranks are cumulated also, down to counts[0] being the failure count for the *worst* training-set performer.

After all replications are complete, in lines 19-20 we divide the counts by the number of replications to get probability of failure for each rank.

At this point we are finished with the essential computation. The remaining lines simply demonstrate how we would likely use this technique. In lines 21-25 we do exactly what we did in lines 8-12, the training phase, except that now we use the entire dataset. In lines 26-27 we print these results in *descending* order of performance. Because we sorted in line 25, we print criters[icomp]. Hopefully now you see why in line 17 we computed counts based on rank, not competitor. We are not so much interested in specific competitors as in the more general concept of *how well high-ranking performance in the training set carries over to above-average performance in the test set*. Thus, counts[icomp] corresponds to the *rank* icomp, not the *competitor* icomp. If you have named or otherwise identified the competitors, the usual case, you must index the name by sort_key to keep the names correctly associated with the other numbers printed.

Optimal Trading Thresholds

On Page 84 we saw a subroutine opt_thresh() that computed upper (long trades) and lower (short trades) thresholds for an indicator such that values satisfying these thresholds triggered trades that maximized profit factor. This subroutine, invoked in lines 10 and 23 of the outline just shown, is usually useful in superiority testing, because you want each competitor to do the best it can. It would be almost pointless to attempt a superiority test if you have just made a guess at an appropriate threshold; you certainly do not want to disadvantage any of the competitors by poor guesswork on your part. Consider the following situations:

- You are screening many different indicators to identify those that are most promising. Each indicator will almost surely have its own optimal threshold.

- You are testing different lookbacks for a single indicator. Unless great care is taken in indicator design, the lookback will affect the distribution of values and hence the optimal threshold.

- You have several different models that make real-valued predictions about future market movement, with greater absolute values indicating greater certainty in the prediction. If these models are fundamentally different, the distributions of their predictions will likely be different, and hence optimal trade thresholds will be different.

- You are testing the same predictive model in different markets. Unless indicators are designed with great care, the same indicator computed from different markets will have different distributions and hence impact the models differently, giving rise to different optimal trade thresholds for the model predictions.

Each replication *must* have its own optimal thresholds computed from the current training set. Do not use the entire dataset to find optimal thresholds once at the start for use throughout the process. Such 'universally superior' thresholds tend to help good competitors more than poor ones, giving rise to optimistic probabilities for the good ones.

Case Study: Optimal Smoothing Lookbacks

This section describes a program that demonstrates use of the superiority algorithm in conjunction with finding the optimal smoothing lookback for an indicator that relies on smoothing to control its wild fluctuations.

The SUP1 directory contains the following files:
    SUP1.CPP - The main program for testing lookback superiority
    RAND.CPP - Random number generator
    QSORTD.CPP - Sorting algorithms
    SPEARMAN.CPP - Compute Spearman rho nonparametric correlation
    OPT_THRESH.CPP - Compute optimal long and short thresholds
    COMP_IND.CPP - Compute the PRICE INTENSITY indicator

The program is called with four parameters:

```
SUP1   S_low   S_high   Nsmooth   Nreps   MarketFile
```

The *S_low* and *S_high* parameters specify the minimum and maximum smoothing lookbacks to test, *Nsmooth* is the number of geometrically spaced lookbacks within these limits, and *Nreps* is the number of trial replications (hundreds or thousands). The *MarketFile* parameter specifies the market history file, each of whose lines specifies the date as YYYYMMDD, the open, high, low, and close. Spaces, tabs, or commas may be used as delimiters. Anything after these prices, such as volume, is ignored. Here are two sample lines from a market history file:

```
19880211 122.32 122.89 121.42 121.92 4015
19880212 121.92 123.37 121.82 122.72 3544
```

The program generates *Nsmooth* competitors geometrically spaced from *S_low* through *S_high*. As final output, for each it computes separate optimal long and short thresholds, printing them along with their profit factors. Then it prints pooled long/short profit factors, sorted from best to worst, along with the superiority 'p-values' for each. Please remember that calling them p-values is a slight stretch; they really are probabilities of failure to outperform the median test-set performance. But in practice they serve very similar purposes, and they are 'probability values'!

The PRICE INTENSITY Indicator

David Bostian invented an indicator called *Intraday Intensity*. It examines intraday price movement as well as the volume that accompanies that price movement. Removing the volume component, which of course changes the nature of the indicator, produces an alternative indicator that captures related information, is easy to normalize, and is a very effective indicator for mean-reversion systems.

The raw (unsmoothed) PRICE INTENSITY indicator for a bar is the open-to-close price change relative to the range of prices for this bar and the close of the prior bar. This is given by Equation (5.1), in which C is the current bar's close, O the open, H the high, and L the low.

$$RAW\ PRICE\ INTENSITY\ =\ \frac{100\,(C-O)}{Max\,[H\text{-}L,\ H\text{-}PriorC,\ PriorC\text{-}L]} \quad (5.1)$$

It should be apparent that the range of this raw indicator is [–100, 100], and that it generally swings wildly up and down. Exponential smoothing is almost always used to tame the gyrations and expose underlying tendencies in intra-bar trends. This is done using the exponential smoothing given by Equation (5.2) with alpha given by Equation (5.3).

$$S_t\ =\ \alpha X_t + (1-\alpha)\,S_{t-1} \quad (5.2)$$

The term *effective lookback* applies to exponential smoothing and determines alpha in that equation. Mathematically, a simple moving average (mean across a moving window) and exponential smoothing are very different, due primarily to the fact that exponential smoothing incorporates every observation ever seen into the smoothed value, not just the values in a window. So how can we talk about the length of an exponential smoothing lookback window, when the lookback is infinite? The short answer (which is all you will get here) is that if a simple moving average has a lookback of k, then exponential smoothing will share several important properties with this simple moving average when alpha is given by Equation (5.3).

$$\alpha\ =\ \frac{2}{(k+1)} \quad (5.3)$$

This indicator is computed in the module COMP_IND.CPP. You can easily substitute your own indicator for this one just by replacing the code in this module. Here is the code for computing this indicator:

```
void comp_ind (
    int n ,              // Number of market price bars
    double *open ,  // They are here
    double *high ,
    double *low ,
    double *close ,
    int iparam ,       // Competition parameter, n to smooth here
    double *ind        // The indicator values are output here
    )
{
    int ibar ;
    double denom, alpha, rawval, smoothed ;

    alpha = 2.0 / (iparam + 1.0) ;   // Exponential smoothing constant; Equation (5.3)

    // Initialize the first indicator value
    denom = high[0] - low[0] ;
    if (denom < 1.e-60)
        denom = 1.e-60 ;
    ind[0] = (close[0] - open[0]) / denom ;
    smoothed = ind[0] ;   // Initialize for smoothing

    for (ibar=1 ; ibar<n ; ibar++) {  // Do the remaining bars

        // Find the max range, the max of these three differences
        denom = high[ibar] - low[ibar] ;        // For Equation (5.1)
        if (high[ibar] - close[ibar-1] > denom)
            denom = high[ibar] - close[ibar-1] ;
        if (close[ibar-1] - low[ibar] > denom)
            denom = close[ibar-1] - low[ibar] ;
        if (denom < 1.e-60)
            denom = 1.e-60 ;

        rawval = (close[ibar] - open[ibar]) / denom ;      // Equation (5.1)
        smoothed = alpha * rawval + (1.0 - alpha) * smoothed ; // Smooth it
        ind[ibar] = 100.0 * smoothed ;    // Multiplier of 100 makes it more human-friendly
        }
}
```

Implementing the Superiority Algorithm

The code presented in this section is extracted from the complete program in SUP1.CPP. I'll skip over the boring task of reading the market history, and jump right into the algorithm that was outlined on Page 134. We begin by computing the market returns and the matrix of competitors. There are nprices bars, but we lose the last one due to the need to look ahead one bar to get the return. Note that the layout of indicator values shown on Page 133 has the observations running down rows, which is how the layout was presented in the Bailey et al paper, but for computational efficiency I use the transpose of this layout, having observations run across columns. The smoothing lookback, param, is computed by simple geometric spacing between the user-specified lower and upper limits, rounded to the nearest integer. The comp_ind() routine which computes the vector of values for a given lookback was listed on the previous page.

```
for (i=0 ; i<nprices-1 ; i++)
  returns[i] = log ( close[i+1] / close[i] ) ;

for (icomp=0 ; icomp<n_smooth ; icomp++) {
  xptr = indicators + icomp * nprices ;   // This competitor's observations
  param = s_low * exp ( icomp / (n_smooth - 1.0) * log ( s_high / s_low ) ) ;
  comp_ind ( nprices , open , high , low , close , (int) (param + 0.5) , xptr ) ;
  }
```

We zero the failure counters and initialize the observation index vector to be an identity. Then we are ready for the replications.

```
for (icomp=0 ; icomp<n_smooth ; icomp++)
  counts[icomp] = 0.0 ;   // Will count failures to exceed median for each rank

for (ibar=0 ; ibar<nprices-1 ; ibar++)
  index[ibar] = ibar ;       // Will index bars

for (irep=0 ; irep<nreps ; irep++) {
```

The first step in a replication is to shuffle the index vector so as to randomly separate the observations into a training set and a test set. We will define the training set to be the first half of this vector.

```
i = nprices-1 ;        // Number remaining to be shuffled
while (i > 1) {        // While at least 2 left to shuffle
  j = (int) (unifrand() * i) ;
  if (j >= i)          // Cheap insurance against disaster if unifrand() returns 1.0
    j = i - 1 ;
  k = index[--i] ;
  index[i] = index[j] ;
  index[j] = k ;
  }
```

We collect in **ret_work** the market returns for the training set, and then we loop through each competitor. For each competitor, first set **sort_key** to be an identity as discussed earlier. Collect in **xwork** the observations for this competitor.

```
for (i=0 ; i<(nprices-1)/2 ; i++) {  // Training set
  k = index[i] ;
  ret_work[i] = returns[k] ;         // Collect returns for training set
  }

for (icomp=0 ; icomp<n_smooth ; icomp++) { // Process each competitor
  sort_key[icomp] = icomp ;                // We'll need this for sorting later
  xptr = indicators + icomp * nprices ;    // This competitor's observations
  for (i=0 ; i<(nprices-1)/2 ; i++) {      // Training set
    k = index[i] ;
    xwork[i] = xptr[k] ;                   // Collect this competitor's training set
    }
```

The next step for this competitor is to ensure that the indicator and the market returns are not negatively correlated. This lets us associate large values with long trades. Then optimize the thresholds. I arbitrarily demand that 10 percent (0.1) of bars produce a trade on each side.

```
rho[icomp] = spearman ( (nprices-1)/2 , xwork , ret_work , work1 , work2 ) ;
if (rho[icomp] < 0.0) {  // For simplicity I demand non-negative correlation
  for (i=0 ; i<(nprices-1)/2 ; i++)
    xwork[i] = -xwork[i] ;
  }

opt_thresh ( (nprices-1)/2 , (int) (0.1 * (nprices-1)/2) , 0 , xwork , ret_work ,
        &pf_all , high_thresh+icomp , &pf_high , low_thresh+icomp , &pf_low ,
        work1 , work2 ) ;  // Described on Page 84
```

We now compute the profit factor for this competitor in the training set. Then, after all competitors have been done, sort the profit factors into ascending order, simultaneously moving their indices in **sort_key**. That way, after sorting, **sort_key[0]** will be the index of the competitor with the worst performance, **sort_key[1]** the second-worst, and so forth.

```
long_win = long_lose = short_win = short_lose = 1.e-60 ;
for (i=0 ; i<(nprices-1)/2 ; i++) {     // Training set
  if (xwork[i] >= high_thresh[icomp]) { // Take a long position?
    if (ret_work[i] > 0.0)
      long_win += ret_work[i] ;
    else
      long_lose -= ret_work[i] ;
    }
  if (xwork[i] < low_thresh[icomp]) { // Take a short position?
    if (ret_work[i] < 0.0)
      short_win -= ret_work[i] ;
    else
      short_lose += ret_work[i] ;
    }
  } // For training set
criters[icomp] = (long_win + short_win) / (long_lose + short_lose) ;
  } // For all competitors

qsortdsi ( 0 , n_smooth-1 , criters , sort_key ) ;
```

We now repeat these operations for the test set, except that we use the previously computed correlation to determine whether we flip the sign of the indicator, and we employ the previously compute thresholds.

```
for (i=(nprices-1)/2 ; i<nprices-1 ; i++) { // Test set
  k = index[i] ;
  ret_work[i] = returns[k] ;                    // Collect returns for test set
  }

for (icomp=0 ; icomp<n_smooth ; icomp++) {
  xptr = indicators + icomp * nprices ;         // This competitor's observations
  for (i=(nprices-1)/2 ; i<nprices-1 ; i++) {   // Test set
    k = index[i] ;
    xwork[i] = xptr[k] ;                         // Collect this competitor for test set
    }
```

```
    if (rho[icomp] < 0.0) {  // If we flipped sign in training, must also in test
      for (i=(nprices-1)/2 ; i<nprices-1 ; i++) // Test set
        xwork[i] = -xwork[i] ;
      }

    long_win = long_lose = short_win = short_lose = 1.e-60 ;
    for (i=(nprices-1)/2 ; i<nprices-1 ; i++) {         // Test set
      if (xwork[i] >= high_thresh[icomp]) {            // Take a long position?
        if (ret_work[i] > 0.0)
          long_win += ret_work[i] ;
        else
          long_lose -= ret_work[i] ;
        }
      if (xwork[i] < low_thresh[icomp]) { // Take a short position?
        if (ret_work[i] < 0.0)
          short_win -= ret_work[i] ;
        else
          short_lose += ret_work[i] ;
        }
      } // For test set

    criters[icomp] = (long_win + short_win) / (long_lose + short_lose) ;
    work1[icomp] = criters[icomp] ;   // We cannot disturb test-set crits, so copy
    } // For all competitors (icomp)

  qsortd ( 0 , n_smooth-1 , work1 ) ;
  if (n_smooth % 2)
    median = work1[n_smooth/2] ;
  else
    median = 0.5 * (work1[n_smooth/2-1] + work1[n_smooth/2]) ;
```

For each training-set rank's competitor (**sort_key[icomp]**), see if its test-set performance fails to exceed the median. This is lines 16-18 on Page 134.

```
  for (icomp=0 ; icomp<n_smooth ; icomp++) {
    if (criters[sort_key[icomp]] <= median)
      ++counts[icomp] ;
    }
  } // For irep

 for (icomp=0 ; icomp<n_smooth ; icomp++)  // Divide to convert counts to probabilities
   counts[icomp] /= nreps ;
```

The essential work is complete. At this time, counts[0] is the probability that the worst training-set competitor will have a test-set performance that fails to exceed the median. Similarly, counts[n_smooth-1] is the probability that the best training-set competitor will have a test-set performance that fails to exceed the median. Thus, we can (roughly speaking) consider these quantities to indicate the likelihood that each ranked performer could have done as well as it did by luck.

This is especially useful information for the high-ranked competitors, those that did well in the training set. If we find that this probability is nicely small (0.05 or even 0.01 are common thresholds) then we can conclude that this high-ranked competitor is truly superior.

As a useful final step we find the performance of each competitor using the entire dataset. We print these, sorted from best to worst, and also print the associated probabilities. We have in counts the failure probabilities for each rank. So when we rank the results for the entire dataset, we can associate these probabilities with the same ranks. In other words, the best performer for the entire dataset will be associated with counts[n_smooth-1] and so forth.

We begin by doing exactly the same thing we did in the training phase of each replication: force the indicator to not have negative correlation with the market returns. Then find the optimal long and short thresholds.

```
for (icomp=0 ; icomp<n_smooth ; icomp++) {
  xptr = indicators + icomp * nprices ;   // This competitor's observations
  param = s_low * exp ( icomp / (n_smooth - 1.0) * log ( s_high / s_low ) ) ;
  rho[icomp] = spearman ( nprices-1 , xptr , returns , work1 , work2 ) ;
  if (rho[icomp] < 0.0) { // For simplicity I demand non-negative correlation
    for (i=0 ; i<nprices-1 ; i++)
      xptr[i] = -xptr[i] ;
    }
  opt_thresh ( nprices-1 , (int) (0.1 * nprices) , 0 , xptr , returns , &pf_all ,
          high_thresh+icomp , &pf_high , low_thresh+icomp , &pf_low ,
          work1 , work2 ) ;
  }
```

Now pass through the dataset, cumulating the wins and losses for profit factor computation.

```
for (icomp=0 ; icomp<n_smooth ; icomp++) {
  sort_key[icomp] = icomp ;
  xptr = indicators + icomp * nprices ;  // This competitor's observations
  long_win = long_lose = short_win = short_lose = 1.e-60 ;
  for (i=0 ; i<nprices-1 ; i++) {
    if (xptr[i] >= high_thresh[icomp]) { // Take a long position?
      if (returns[i] > 0.0)
        long_win += returns[i] ;
      else
        long_lose -= returns[i] ;
      }
    if (xptr[i] < low_thresh[icomp]) { // Take a short position?
      if (returns[i] < 0.0)
        short_win -= returns[i] ;
      else
        short_lose += returns[i] ;
      }
    } // For training set
  criters[icomp] = (long_win + short_win) / (long_lose + short_lose) ;
  } // For all competitors
```

All that's left to do is sort the performance criteria in ascending order and print them from last (best) to first (worst). Remember that icomp here is referring to rank, not the competitor indices. These we have to get via sort_key.

```
qsortdsi ( 0 , n_smooth-1 , criters , sort_key ) ;

for (icomp=n_smooth-1 ; icomp>=0 ; icomp--) { // Best to worst
  k = sort_key[icomp] ;
  param = s_low * exp ( k / (n_smooth - 1.0) * log ( s_high / s_low ) ) ;
  // Print here: (int) (param + 0.5), criters[icomp], counts[icomp] ) ;
  }
```

Demonstrating the SUP1 Program

I ran the SUP1 program on OEX from early 1988 through late 2019. There were 10 competing smoothing lookbacks ranging from 1 through 200, and I used 10,000 replications. The following output was generated:

Parameter	Correl	Long thresh	Long pf	Short thresh	Short pf
1	-0.0469	74.58609	1.436	-82.41242	1.024
2	-0.0529	49.69356	1.604	-57.96962	1.198
3	-0.0545	38.11840	1.581	-45.29014	1.119
6	-0.0562	23.90934	1.636	-27.70091	1.155
11	-0.0552	16.07269	1.456	-18.90653	1.136
19	-0.0507	11.19972	1.429	-11.46074	1.054
34	-0.0412	7.13930	1.301	-16.93764	1.005
62	-0.0278	3.53762	1.202	-13.30774	0.969
111	-0.0152	-4.07056	1.109	-12.25173	1.055
200	-0.0056	-3.11676	1.107	-10.72777	1.061

Competitor performance ranked best to worst, with superiority 'p-values' (failure rates)

Parameter	Profit factor	p-value
2	1.434	0.036
6	1.396	0.086
3	1.375	0.120
11	1.291	0.233
1	1.246	0.348
34	1.211	0.570
19	1.199	0.789
62	1.126	0.907
111	1.102	0.948
200	1.099	0.961

Note that the PRICE INTENSITY indicator is negatively correlated with market returns for all smoothing lookbacks, so understand that the long and short thresholds refer to the *negative* of the indicator.

We see that this indicator clearly prefers short smoothing lookbacks, although it does not like a lookback of 1, which means no smoothing (just use the raw value). The best smoothing lookback, 2, has a nicely but not extremely small failure rate of 0.036. This means that in the replications, whichever competitor had the best training-set performance had only this small probability of having test-set performance greater than the median. Since in the entire dataset a lookback of 2 was the best, we assign it this probability. I call this failure rate a p-value; it really isn't, but the similarity is close enough that I am comfortable doing so.

Case Study: Indicator Performance Across Markets

In the prior section, which you should be familiar with before embarking on this section, I presented an example of using the superiority algorithm to compare different smoothing lookbacks for the PRICE INTENSITY indicator. In this section I use this algorithm to compare how this indicator, with a fixed lookback of 2, performs across a wide variety of markets.

The SUP2 directory contains the following files:
    SUP2.CPP - The main program for testing market superiority
    RAND.CPP - Random number generator
    QSORTD.CPP - Sorting algorithms
    SPEARMAN.CPP - Compute Spearman rho nonparametric correlation
    OPT_THRESH.CPP - Compute optimal long and short thresholds
    COMP_IND.CPP - Compute the PRICE INTENSITY indicator

The program is called with three parameters:

```
SUP2  Nsmooth  Nreps  MarketListName
```

Nsmooth is the indicator's smoothing lookback parameter, and *Nreps* is the number of trial replications (hundreds or thousands). The *MarketListName* is an ordinary text file that gives the full path names of the markets to test. Here are the first few lines of the market list file that I use in an example later:

```
E:\MorningStar\MG110.txt
E:\MorningStar\MG111.txt
E:\MorningStar\MG112.txt
```

Each market history file must be one bar per line, with the date as YYYYMMDD, the open, high, low, and close. Spaces, tabs, or commas may be used as delimiters. Anything after these prices, such as volume, is ignored. Here are two sample lines from a market history file:

```
19880211 122.32 122.89 121.42 121.92 4015
19880212 121.92 123.37 121.82 122.72 3544
```

The program generates a competitor for each market. As final output, for each it will compute separate optimal long and short thresholds, printing them along with their profit factors. Then it prints a table of pooled long/short profit factors, sorted from best to worst, along with the superiority 'p-values' (failure rates) for each.

Implementing the Superiority Algorithm

This section is almost a waste of paper, because it is so similar to the implementation in the prior section. However, in that section we used one market with multiple competing parameters, while in this section we use one parameter with multiple competing markets. This gives rise to a few significant differences in implementation, so I will run through it quickly, focusing on the differences, trusting that the reader is already familiar enough with the basics from the prior section that detailed explanations are not needed.

As before, I'll ignore the mundane details of reading the market histories. This code is in SUP2.CPP. At this point we have n_markets market histories, each containing n_bars bars of price data. The program ensured that all prices are aligned, so that a bar at a given offset in all markets refers to the same date. The first step is to compute the market returns, as usual the log of the price change ratio. Note that we cannot compute the return for the last bar because we have to look one bar ahead to get a return.

```
for (imarket=0 ; imarket<n_markets ; imarket++) {
   for (ibar=0 ; ibar<n_bars-1 ; ibar++)
     returns[imarket*n_bars+ibar] = log ( market_close[imarket][ibar+1] /
                                          market_close[imarket][ibar] ) ;
   }
```

Next we compute the matrix of indicator values. Unlike in the prior section, now we have to use a separate market history for each competitor; we will compute the indicators from the same market whose returns we will evaluate. Theoretically they need not be the same, and it may occasionally be useful to employ prices in one market to trade a different market. But that doesn't happen very often!

```
for (imarket=0 ; imarket<n_markets ; imarket++) {
  xptr = indicators + imarket * n_bars ;   // This competitor's observations
  comp_ind ( n_bars , market_open[imarket] , market_high[imarket] ,
       market_low[imarket] , market_close[imarket] , lookback , xptr ) ;
  }
```

We zero the failure counters and initialize the observation index vector to
be an identity. Then we are ready for the replications. The first step in a
replication is to shuffle the index vector that defines the training and test
sets. Recall that we lost the last bar due to the need to look ahead one bar
for returns.

```
for (imarket=0 ; imarket<n_markets ; imarket++)
  counts[imarket] = 0.0 ;  // Will count failures to exceed median for each rank

for (ibar=0 ; ibar<n_bars-1 ; ibar++)
  index[ibar] = ibar ;   // Will index bars

for (irep=0 ; irep<nreps ; irep++) {

  i = n_bars-1 ;    // Number remaining to be shuffled; Last price lost from lookahead
  while (i > 1) { // While at least 2 left to shuffle
    j = (int) (unifrand() * i) ;
    if (j >= i)  // Cheap insurance against disaster if unifrand() returns 1.0
      j = i - 1 ;
    k = index[--i] ;
    index[i] = index[j] ;
    index[j] = k ;
    }
```

We find the training-set criterion for each competitor, and then we sort
them ascending, simultaneously moving a sort key. The first step
processing the training set is collecting the training set data. We must fetch
the returns inside the competitor loop, because markets are competing. (In
the prior section we were able to do this outside the loop because all
competitors used the same market.) For each competitor we find its
Spearman correlation with the returns. If it is negatively correlated, flip its
sign. I arbitrarily demand that at least 10 percent (0.1) of bars have a trade.
Feel free to change this or make it a user parameter, but 0.1 generally
works well.

```
for (imarket=0 ; imarket<n_markets ; imarket++) { // Process each competitor
  sort_key[imarket] = imarket ;

  for (i=0 ; i<(n_bars-1)/2 ; i++) {                    // Training set
    k = index[i] ;
    ret_work[i] = returns[imarket*n_bars+k] ;   // Collect returns for training set
    }

  xptr = indicators + imarket * n_bars ;        // This competitor's observations
  for (i=0 ; i<(n_bars-1)/2 ; i++) {            // Training set
    k = index[i] ;
    xwork[i] = xptr[k] ;                        // Collect competitor for training set
    }

  rho[imarket] = spearman ( (n_bars-1)/2 , xwork , ret_work , work1 , work2 ) ;
  if (rho[imarket] < 0.0) {  // For simplicity I demand non-negative correlation
    for (i=0 ; i<(n_bars-1)/2 ; i++)
      xwork[i] = -xwork[i] ;
    }

  opt_thresh ( (n_bars-1)/2 , (int) (0.1 * (n_bars-1)/2) , 0 , xwork , ret_work ,
          &pf_all , high_thresh+imarket , &pf_high , low_thresh+imarket , &pf_low ,
          work1 , work2 ) ;

  long_win = long_lose = short_win = short_lose = 1.e-60 ;
  for (i=0 ; i<(n_bars-1)/2 ; i++) {          // Training set
    if (xwork[i] >= high_thresh[imarket]) { // Take a long position?
      if (ret_work[i] > 0.0)
        long_win += ret_work[i] ;
      else
        long_lose -= ret_work[i] ;
      }
    if (xwork[i] < low_thresh[imarket]) {    // Take a short position?
      if (ret_work[i] < 0.0)
        short_win -= ret_work[i] ;
      else
        short_lose += ret_work[i] ;
      }
    } // For training set
  criters[imarket] = (long_win + short_win) / (long_lose + short_lose) ;
  } // For all competitors

qsortdsi ( 0 , n_markets-1 , criters , sort_key ) ;
```

Now we find the test-set criterion for each competitor, using the thresholds and possible flipped sign determined from the training set. When all competitors are done, find the median test-set return.

```
for (imarket=0 ; imarket<n_markets ; imarket++) {
  for (i=(n_bars-1)/2 ; i<n_bars-1 ; i++) {        // Test set
    k = index[i] ;
    ret_work[i] = returns[imarket*n_bars+k] ;   // Collect returns for test set
    }
  xptr = indicators + imarket * n_bars ;          // This competitor's observations
  for (i=(n_bars-1)/2 ; i<n_bars-1 ; i++) {        // Test set
    k = index[i] ;
    xwork[i] = xptr[k] ;                          // Collect this competitor for test set
    }
  if (rho[imarket] < 0.0) {  // If we flipped sign in training, must also in test
    for (i=(n_bars-1)/2 ; i<n_bars-1 ; i++)        // Test set
      xwork[i] = -xwork[i] ;
    }
  long_win = long_lose = short_win = short_lose = 1.e-60 ;
  for (i=(n_bars-1)/2 ; i<n_bars-1 ; i++) { // Test set
    if (xwork[i] >= high_thresh[imarket]) { // Take a long position?
      if (ret_work[i] > 0.0)
        long_win += ret_work[i] ;
      else
        long_lose -= ret_work[i] ;
      }
    if (xwork[i] < low_thresh[imarket]) { // Take a short position?
      if (ret_work[i] < 0.0)
        short_win -= ret_work[i] ;
      else
        short_lose += ret_work[i] ;
      }
    } // For test set
  criters[imarket] = (long_win + short_win) / (long_lose + short_lose) ;
  work1[imarket] = criters[imarket] ;   // We cannot disturb test-set crits
  } // For all competitors

qsortd ( 0 , n_markets-1 , work1 ) ;
if (n_markets % 2)
  median = work1[n_markets/2] ;
else
  median = 0.5 * (work1[n_markets/2-1] + work1[n_markets/2]) ;
```

The last step in a replication is counting failures. For each training-set rank, see if its test-set criterion fails to exceed the median of all test-set criteria. Then divide the counts by number of replications to make them probabilities.

```
for (imarket=0 ; imarket<n_markets ; imarket++) {
  if (criters[sort_key[imarket]] <= median)
    ++counts[imarket] ;
  }
} // For irep

for (imarket=0 ; imarket<n_markets ; imarket++)
  counts[imarket] /= nreps ;
```

We finish up with the same optional but very useful code that we employed in the prior section. Process the entire dataset, finding optimal thresholds and possibly flipping indicator signs to prevent negative correlation with the market returns. This information is nice to print for the user. Then sort performances and print them in descending order, associating with each rank the corresponding failure probability in counts. Here is the 'training' code.

```
for (imarket=0 ; imarket<n_markets ; imarket++) {
  xptr = indicators + imarket * n_bars ;   // This competitor's observations
  rho[imarket] = spearman ( n_bars-1 , xptr , returns+imarket*n_bars , work1 , work2 );
  if (rho[imarket] < 0.0) {  // For simplicity I demand non-negative correlation
    for (i=0 ; i<n_bars-1 ; i++)
      xptr[i] = -xptr[i] ;
    }
  opt_thresh ( n_bars-1 , (int) (0.1 * n_bars) , 0 , xptr , returns+imarket*n_bars ,
          &pf_all , high_thresh+imarket , &pf_high , low_thresh+imarket , &pf_low ,
          work1 , work2 ) ;
  // Print market names, correlations, thresholds, and profit factors here
  }
```

All that's left is to compute the performances, sort them in descending order, and print them. Note how we use sort_key to associate the market name with the other results correctly.

```
for (imarket=0 ; imarket<n_markets ; imarket++) {
  sort_key[imarket] = imarket ;
  xptr = indicators + imarket * n_bars ;  // This competitor's observations
  ret_ptr = returns + imarket * n_bars ;  // This competitor's market returns
  long_win = long_lose = short_win = short_lose = 1.e-60 ;
  for (i=0 ; i<n_bars-1 ; i++) {
    if (xptr[i] >= high_thresh[imarket]) { // Take a long position?
      if (ret_ptr[i] > 0.0)
        long_win += ret_ptr[i] ;
      else
        long_lose -= ret_ptr[i] ;
      }
    if (xptr[i] < low_thresh[imarket]) { // Take a short position?
      if (ret_ptr[i] < 0.0)
        short_win -= ret_ptr[i] ;
      else
        short_lose += ret_ptr[i] ;
      }
    } // For training set
  criters[imarket] = (long_win + short_win) / (long_lose + short_lose) ;
  } // For all competitors

qsortdsi ( 0 , n_markets-1 , criters , sort_key ) ;

// Print competitors in descending order of performance
for (imarket=n_markets-1 ; imarket>=0 ; imarket--) {  // Best to worst
  k = sort_key[imarket] ;
  // Print market_names[k], criters[imarket], counts[imarket] ) ;
  }
```

It's important to understand those last few lines. The loop variable imarket
does not directly refer to markets, but rather to *ranks*. The value 0 refers to
the *worst* performing market, while n_markets-1 is the best performer. We
have sorted criters, so those values will be printed in descending order.
We computed counts to be based on ranks, not markets, with counts[0]
being the failure rate for the worst performer and counts[n_markets-1]
being that for the best. But the sorting operation disconnected the criteria
from the competitors' names. This is why we used sort_key to keep track
of the rearrangement, enabling us to reconnect them.

Demonstrating the SUP2 Program

I ran the SUP2 program using 221 MorningStar market sector indices, those that (to the best of my knowledge) covered 1988 through 2019 with no interruptions. Since I already knew that for OEX the best smoothing lookback is 2, that is what I used for this test. I used 10,000 replications to get extreme accuracy. My first surprise was that, unlike the case for OEX, over 3/4 of these markets had positive correlation between the indicator and the market return. Here are the first few lines of the threshold analysis:

```
Market Correl Long thresh    Long pf   Short thresh  Short pf
MG110  0.0361    35.19652     1.372      -24.49895     1.252
MG111  0.0232    37.64314     1.287      -16.35565     1.107
MG112  0.0197    35.96802     1.194      -20.73384     1.147
MG113  0.0344    34.85674     1.290      -34.12879     1.213
MG114  0.0294    23.70272     1.308      -20.88415     1.092
MG120  0.0501    24.73648     1.311      -31.95951     1.181
MG121 -0.0134    27.12346     1.198      -40.56682     1.114
MG122  0.0571    37.33094     1.345      -30.61550     1.237
```

The other surprise was how one sector (jewelry stores) stood out from the others, as shown in the first few lines of the final result shown below. Please do remember that this test does not measure absolute quality; I would like to see a walkforward equity curve, along with a permutation test of the out-of-sample returns. This test measures only superiority relative to peers. So it's possible for a *nearly* worthless model or indicator to stand out when all of its competitors are *completely* worthless. Also remember that these profit factors are optimistically biased due to the long and short thresholds being optimized. Still, this result got my attention!

```
Market     Profit factor     p-value
MG743          1.958          0.003
MG416          1.714          0.028
MG334          1.455          0.118
MG126          1.454          0.142
MG426          1.418          0.153
MG134          1.404          0.161
MG130          1.397          0.160
MG754          1.393          0.173
MG814          1.392          0.173
MG720          1.386          0.173
MG712          1.378          0.181
MG621          1.365          0.182
MG726          1.362          0.188
```

I was curious to see if I got this result simply from having examined such a vast number of competitors. In theory this test should be quite robust against selection bias, so the chance of one market standing out so strongly by sheer good luck should be tiny. Nonetheless, I was inspired to use a smoothing lookback of 500, which is so huge as to remove nearly all predictive information. I ran the same test, but with a lookback of 500 instead of 2. Here are the beginning lines of this output. The results are exactly what one would expect with a worthless indicator: the p-values are randomly distributed around central values, with no p-values that are extremely large or small. By the way, don't conclude that there is a net bias for p-values to be above 0.5. Later in this long list values around 0.4 become common. This sort of antithetical behavior often happens when an indicator-target relationship is anti-predictive, meaning that with a finite dataset, in-sample behavior tends to run opposite out-of-sample behavior. It's a fascinating phenomenon somewhat related to the famous no-free-lunch theorems.

Market	Profit factor	p-value
MG345	1.214	0.673
MG448	1.206	0.600
MG627	1.204	0.622
MG914	1.188	0.626
MG736	1.186	0.568
MG847	1.185	0.610
MG850	1.181	0.602
MG771	1.176	0.582
MG853	1.174	0.620
MG449	1.170	0.603
MG845	1.170	0.575
MG527	1.167	0.614
MG526	1.164	0.599
MG913	1.157	0.618
MG315	1.154	0.596
MG832	1.149	0.594
MG635	1.146	0.591
MG724	1.144	0.584
MG774	1.143	0.614
MG318	1.143	0.590
MG775	1.142	0.571
MG843	1.141	0.566
MG611	1.140	0.595
MG842	1.139	0.598
MG751	1.139	0.573
MG837	1.139	0.565
MG759	1.136	0.573
MG723	1.134	0.577

Case Study: Optimal Holding Period

In the first of these three case studies, which you should be familiar with before embarking on this section, I presented an example of using the superiority algorithm to compare different smoothing lookbacks for the PRICE INTENSITY indicator. In the second I showed how to use an indicator in multiple competing markets to find the market that is best predicted by the indicator. In this section I use this algorithm to find the optimal holding period for a position signaled by an indicator. To summarize these three examples:

Case 1: Next bar change in a market, with competing indicators defined by varying the indicator's parameter. The *indicators* are competing.

Case 2: Next bar change signaled by one indicator evaluated in multiple competing markets. The *markets* are competing.

Case 3: Single market, single indicator, with different holding periods competing. The *holding periods* are competing.

The SUP3 directory contains the following files:
   SUP3.CPP - The main program for testing holding-period superiority
   RAND.CPP - Random number generator
   QSORTD.CPP - Sorting algorithms
   SPEARMAN.CPP - Compute Spearman rho nonparametric correlation
   OPT_THRESH.CPP - Compute optimal long and short thresholds
   COMP_IND.CPP - Compute the PRICE INTENSITY indicator

The program is called with six parameters:

```
SUP3 Nsmooth LookLow LookHigh Detrend Nreps MarketFile
```

Nsmooth is the PRICE INTENSITY indicator's smoothing lookback parameter, and *Nreps* is the number of trial replications (hundreds or thousands). It will test lookahead distances (holding periods) from *LookLow* through *LookHigh*. If Detrend is 0 the actual market returns are used, while if it is nonzero the effect of trend interacting with positions is eliminated. This is discussed soon.

The *MarketFile* parameter specifies the market history file, each of whose lines specifies the date as YYYYMMDD, the open, high, low, and close. Spaces, tabs, or commas may be used as delimiters. Anything after these prices, such as volume, is ignored. Here are two sample lines from a market history file:

```
19880211 122.32 122.89 121.42 121.92 4015
19880212 121.92 123.37 121.82 122.72 3544
```

The program generates a competitor for each holding period. As final output, for each it will compute separate optimal long and short thresholds, printing them along with their profit factors. Then it prints a table of pooled long/short profit factors, sorted from best to worst, along with the superiority 'p-values' (failure rates) for each.

Thoughts on Holding Period Analysis

Nearly all studies in this book employ returns based on looking ahead one bar. There is a reason for this, based on my decades of financial market research. I have found, almost without exception, that any indicator or predictive model makes its most reliable predictions for the market move to the *next* bar, a holding period of one bar. Also, as I'll explain soon, there are other practical as well as theoretical benefits to looking ahead just one bar when doing a statistical study. Thus, reevaluating an indicator on each bar in order to always have its most recent value, and relating this value to the move to the next bar, is an excellent way to measure the predictive power of an indicator. And in practice it is very often an excellent way to conduct real-life trading.

But sometimes, when we are trading real money rather than doing theoretical analyses, we may want to look ahead more than one bar, or at least ponder some theoretical results related to longer holding periods. In other words, we may want our return to be defined as the *sum* of a number of future one-bar moves. Why would we do this when much experience indicates that the most reliable predictions are just one bar ahead?

The reason becomes apparent when we consider *risk-adjusted* returns. (It should come as no surprise to readers that my favored risk-adjust return for this test is profit factor!) The predictive power of a good indicator or model fades as we move into the future, but it often does so fairly slowly. So when we look ahead two bars, and three, and four, we have less and less of the directional tendency indicated by the prediction, while the noise level remains the same. But random noise tends to cancel, moving prices up one bar and down another, while the predicted directional tendency reinforces from bar to bar, though with less and less impact. So often, for a little while, our return-to-noise ratio improves as we hold the position longer. It may be, for example, that if we hold a position for, say, 5 bars, the reinforced predicted directional tendency will overshadow the moderately canceling random noise over those 5 bars, giving us a larger return relative to noise than we would get from holding the position for just one bar.

Of course, we cannot take this too far. Sooner or later the force of the predicted movement will wane to insignificance, while the noise will continue unabated. Thus, our risk-adjust return, after peaking, will wane due to the risk rising while the return no longer increases.

Our trading system may have its own rule for exiting a position. This may lead us to believe that it makes no difference what some theoretically optimal holding period may be. But surely we should care if our rule results in an average holding period that is very different from the theoretically optimal holding period. So even if our trading system is not based on a fixed, pre-ordained holding period, we should be interested in the optimal holding period.

It is useful to plot a graph of the risk-adjusted return as a function of the lookahead distance. As a general rule, a high-quality indicator or predictive model will have a curve that displays one of two shapes. If the predictive power has a very short life, the risk-adjusted return will peak at a holding period of one bar and drop off after that. If, on the other hand, the predictive power drops more slowly, the curve will start at a moderate level, steadily increase to a peak as the lookahead (holding period) increases, and then drop thereafter.

We may sometimes see several clear peaks in the curve. This may be random effects, or it may be that the predictive model or indicator is responding to several independent properties of the market, and these peaks are due to these properties. But there are two curve shapes that should always make us wary. If the curve does not have one or a very few prominent peaks, but rather bounces around over a long range of lookaheads, this is evidence that the indicator or model is contributing little information to overcome the inherent noise in the market. If, on the other hand, the curve does display a prominent peak, but one that is extremely narrow, we should suspect that either the effect we are seeing is just due to random good luck (the most common culprit), or that the predictive power of the model or indicator is far too selective to be useful (not a common situation).

Caveats

To begin, let's consider why I use just one-bar-ahead returns in all other studies in this book, as well as in nearly all of my other books. Multiple-bar holding periods have at least two major drawbacks.

The first problem is statistical. Nearly every statistical test has the vital assumption that the dependent variable, returns in the case of most trading system tests, are independent. But multiple-bar returns are far from that. For example, suppose we are considering a holding period of 10 bars. In other words, our computed return is the sum of the one-bar returns over the next 10 bars, or equivalently, the change from the current bar to the bar 10 ahead. When we move ahead to the next bar, the 10-bar return for that bar will share 9 individual returns with the net return of the prior bar. This induces such massive serial correlation that all but the most rare and special statistical tests are completely invalidated.

The other problem is practical. In real life we would almost never want to build and close positions that can become potentially large over a long holding period. For example, suppose we find that the optimal holding period is 10 bars, and suppose our indicator or model tells us to take a position. Then suppose that on the next bar we are again told to take a position. And again, and again. This is not unusual, because indicators and model predictions generally change only slowly. We can end up with 10 positions open simultaneously, an outcome that would probably make most traders nervous. So multiple-bar holding periods generally are not reflective of practical, real-life situations.

But for the purposes of this superiority test, neither of these issues presents a problem. We cannot relate computed profit factors to realistically attainable results, nor can we perform other statistical tests on net returns. But our superiority test works fine.

There are two potentially troublesome issues that I will not address in the example that I present later but that I'll discuss here to give the developer a heads-up. The first is that for many models or indicators, trades on the long side will have a significantly different optimal holding period from trades on the short side. For this reason it is often in our best interest to perform two separate superiority tests, one long only and one short only. Of course there is nothing illegal or necessarily bad about combining the two sides into a single test as I do in the example that comes later. In fact, we may want to find the optimal holding period and degree of superiority for our trading system considered as a whole, long and short combined. That's fine. It's just that we can often gain more information by looking at the two sides separately. If, as is often the case, we find that the long and short sides have significantly different optimal holding periods we might want to consider splitting our trading system into two separate systems.

If we do look at one side only, or if we combine both but there is a significant imbalance in the number of long and short positions, there is a truly serious issue that can arise. Suppose, for example, that the market has a substantial long-term upward trend (not uncommon!) and also suppose that we are trading a long-only system (also not uncommon!). Individual bar returns will randomly change from positive to negative and back, with positive somewhat but not overwhelmingly favored. But if we were to have a holding period of, say, 50 bars we would probably find that a large majority of returns are positive, because in most 50-bar blocks the net upward trend would cause positive bar moves to somewhat overshadow negative bar moves over the holding period. As a result, profit factor (as well as many other performance measures) would be dominated by wins, even if the underlying trading system were completely worthless. The combination of the system being long-only, plus most 50-bar returns being positive, would produce a sham 'winning' system.

In some other situations this is not necessarily a bad thing, because one philosophy of market trading says that being long-only in a market that trends upward is intelligent on its own. But when we are in a competition situation as we are here, and a competitor gains an unfair advantage by means of having a long holding period, we are in trouble. In such a case we are liable to find that the performance-versus-lookahead curve heads upward and never turns back as the holding period increases. The more we increase the holding period, the better our apparent results are. This is bad.

The cure is simple. We compute the indicator (or model predictions) based on the original market. Nothing changes there. But for each competitor we compute its mean per-bar return across the entire history. Then, for finding optimal thresholds or evaluating performance, when we compute the profit factor or whatever performance measure we want, we subtract that mean return from the return of each bar. This removes any contribution of trend to the performance measure. It does introduce some generally modest distortions into the results and hence might not always be a good choice. But if you find that your performance-versus-lookahead curve blows up, you absolutely must do this.

My own habit is to do trend elimination by default, just in case. It has been my experience that if a strong trend/position interaction is not present, results are practically the same with and without trend elimination. And if strong interaction is present, trend elimination makes the difference between great results and worthless results. So, in my opinion, with trend elimination you have very little to lose and much to gain. SUP3 allows this option, and I recommend using it.

Implementing the Superiority Algorithm

As before, I'll ignore the mundane details of reading the market history file. This code is in SUP3.CPP. At the point where this discussion begins we have a market history containing n_bars bars of price data. The first step is to compute the market returns, as usual the log of the price change ratio. In the two prior case studies we used a fixed holding period, looking ahead one bar. But here we need a matrix of returns, with a separate series of returns for each lookahead distance. Note that we can compute returns for only n_bars–look_high bars because we have to look ahead to get a return, and we will be looking ahead a maximum of look_high bars for the final competitor. We also compute the mean return for each competitor.

```
for (icomp=look_low ; icomp<=look_high ; icomp++) { // User's range of lookaheads
  k = icomp - look_low ;
  ret_ptr = returns + k * n_bars ;        // This competitor's return series
  mean_rets[k] = 0.0 ;
  for (i=0 ; i<n_bars-look_high ; i++) {
    ret_ptr[i] = log ( close[i+icomp] / close[i] ) ;
    mean_rets[k] += ret_ptr[i] ;
    }
  mean_rets[k] /= n_bars-look_high ;
  }
```

In the two prior examples, each competitor had its own set of indicators. But in this example we have just one fixed indicator vector, based on the original market history. We compute it in the line shown below. As in the prior examples we initialize the failure counters to zero and initialize the case index vector to be an identity vector. Then we begin the replication loop. The first step in that loop is to shuffle the case index vector.

```
comp_ind ( n_bars , open , high , low , close , n_smooth , indicators ) ;

for (icomp=0 ; icomp<n_looks ; icomp++)
  counts[icomp] = 0.0 ;  // Will count failures to exceed median

for (ibar=0 ; ibar<n_bars-look_high ; ibar++)
  index[ibar] = ibar ;   // Will index bars

for (irep=0 ; irep<nreps ; irep++) {
```

```
i = n_bars-look_high ;  // Number remaining to be shuffled
while (i > 1) {              // While at least 2 left to shuffle
  j = (int) (unifrand() * i) ;
  if (j >= i)                // Cheap insurance against disaster if unifrand() returns 1.0
    j = i - 1 ;
  k = index[--i] ;
  index[i] = index[j] ;
  index[j] = k ;
  }
```

We collect both the indicators and the returns inside the competitor (icomp) loop. We do the former because every competitor uses the same indicator set, but it may happen that we flip the sign of a competitor's indicator vector to prevent it from being negatively correlated with the return for that competitor. We do the latter because each competitor has a different return vector (the whole point of this example). Then compute the nonparametric correlation between the indicator and the return. Flip the sign of the indicator if the correlation is negative. Finally, find the optimal trading thresholds (long and short).

```
for (icomp=0 ; icomp<n_looks ; icomp++) {     // Process each competitor
  sort_key[icomp] = icomp ;

  for (i=0 ; i<(n_bars-look_high)/2 ; i++) {       // Training set
    k = index[i] ;
    xwork[i] = indicators[k] ;                       // Collect indicator for training set
    ret_work[i] = returns[icomp*n_bars+k] ;          // Collect returns for training set
    if (trend_elim)                                  // Does user want trend removed?
      ret_work[i] -= mean_rets[icomp] ;
    }

  rho[icomp] = spearman ( (n_bars-look_high)/2 , xwork , ret_work , work1 , work2 ) ;
  if (rho[icomp] < 0.0) {  // For simplicity I demand non-negative correlation
    for (i=0 ; i<(n_bars-look_high)/2 ; i++)
      xwork[i] = -xwork[i] ;
    }

  opt_thresh ( (n_bars-look_high)/2 , (int) (0.1 * (n_bars-look_high)/2) , 0 ,
               xwork , ret_work , &pf_all , high_thresh+icomp , &pf_high ,
               low_thresh+icomp , &pf_low , work1 , work2 ) ;
```

The last step in the 'training' section is to compute the performance criterion for this optimized decision process. If the user has asked for the effect of trend to be eliminated (**trend_elim**), we already subtracted the mean return from each individual return before computing the profit factor, both in the optimization code above and in the performance computation code here. Then sort the criteria ascending, simultaneously moving the indices in **sort_keys**.

```
long_win = long_lose = short_win = short_lose = 1.e-60 ;
for (i=0 ; i<(n_bars-look_high)/2 ; i++) {     // Training set
  ret_val = ret_work[i] ;
  if (xwork[i] >= high_thresh[icomp]) {   // Take a long position?
    if (ret_val > 0.0)
      long_win += ret_val ;
    else
      long_lose -= ret_val ;
    }
  if (xwork[i] < low_thresh[icomp]) {     // Take a short position?
    if (ret_val < 0.0)
      short_win -= ret_val ;
    else
      short_lose += ret_val ;
    }
  } // For training set
criters[icomp] = (long_win + short_win) / (long_lose + short_lose) ;
  } // For all competitors

qsortdsi ( 0 , n_looks-1 , criters , sort_key ) ;
```

Now process the test set, using the optimal thresholds just computed, and flipping the sign of the indicators if we did it during optimization.

```
for (icomp=0 ; icomp<n_looks ; icomp++) {

  for (i=(n_bars-look_high)/2 ; i<n_bars-look_high ; i++) { // Test set
    k = index[i] ;
    xwork[i] = indicators[k] ;                // Collect indicator for test set
    ret_work[i] = returns[icomp*n_bars+k] ;   // Collect returns for test set
    if (trend_elim)
      ret_work[i] -= mean_rets[icomp] ;
    }
```

```
if (rho[icomp] < 0.0) {  // If we flipped sign in training, must also in test
   for (i=(n_bars-look_high)/2 ; i<n_bars-look_high ; i++) // Test set
      xwork[i] = -xwork[i] ;
   }

long_win = long_lose = short_win = short_lose = 1.e-60 ;
for (i=(n_bars-look_high)/2 ; i<n_bars-look_high ; i++) { // Test set
   ret_val = ret_work[i] ;
   if (xwork[i] >= high_thresh[icomp]) {   // Take a long position?
      if (ret_val > 0.0)
         long_win += ret_val ;
      else
         long_lose -= ret_val ;
      }
   if (xwork[i] < low_thresh[icomp]) {      // Take a short position?
      if (ret_val < 0.0)
         short_win -= ret_val ;
      else
         short_lose += ret_val ;
      }
   } // For test set

criters[icomp] = (long_win + short_win) / (long_lose + short_lose) ;
work1[icomp] = criters[icomp] ;    // We cannot disturb test-set crits, so sort this
} // For all competitors
```

Finally, count failures to exceed the median and divide to get probabilities.

```
qsortd ( 0 , n_looks-1 , work1 ) ;
if (n_looks % 2)
   median = work1[n_looks/2] ;
else
   median = 0.5 * (work1[n_looks/2-1] + work1[n_looks/2]) ;

for (icomp=0 ; icomp<n_looks ; icomp++) {     // Count failures at each rank
   if (criters[sort_key[icomp]] <= median)
      ++counts[icomp] ;
   }
} // For irep

for (icomp=0 ; icomp<n_looks ; icomp++)
   counts[icomp] /= nreps ;
```

The important work is done. Now process the entire dataset exactly as we did for the 'training' half before.

```
for (icomp=0 ; icomp<n_looks ; icomp++) {
  for (i=0 ; i<n_bars-look_high ; i++) {
    xwork[i] = indicators[i] ;
    ret_work[i] = returns[icomp*n_bars+i] ;
    if (trend_elim)
      ret_work[i] -= mean_rets[icomp] ;
    }

  rho[icomp] = spearman ( n_bars-look_high , indicators , ret_work , work1 , work2 ) ;
  if (rho[icomp] < 0.0) {  // For simplicity I demand non-negative correlation
    for (i=0 ; i<n_bars-look_high ; i++)
      xwork[i] = -xwork[i] ;
    }

  opt_thresh ( n_bars-look_high , (int) (0.1 * (n_bars-look_high)) , 0 , xwork , ret_work ,
        &pf_all , high_thresh+icomp , &pf_high , low_thresh+icomp , &pf_low ,
        work1 , work2 ) ;
  // Print thresholds and profit factors here
  }
```

For each competitor, pass through the entire dataset, computing its performance criterion.

```
for (icomp=0 ; icomp<n_looks ; icomp++) {
  sort_key[icomp] = icomp ;   // Will preserve indices of each rank after sorting

  for (i=0 ; i<n_bars-look_high ; i++) {
    xwork[i] = indicators[i] ;
    ret_work[i] = returns[icomp*n_bars+i] ;
    if (trend_elim)     // Eliminate trend if user requested it
      ret_work[i] -= mean_rets[icomp] ;
    }

  if (rho[icomp] < 0.0) {   // Flip indicator sign if needed to prevent negative correlation
    for (i=0 ; i<n_bars-look_high ; i++)
      xwork[i] = -xwork[i] ;
    }

  ret_ptr = returns + icomp * n_bars ;
```

```
long_win = long_lose = short_win = short_lose = 1.e-60 ;

for (i=0 ; i<n_bars-look_high ; i++) {
  ret_val = ret_ptr[i] ;

  if (xwork[i] >= high_thresh[icomp]) {      // Take a long position?
    if (ret_val > 0.0)
      long_win += ret_val ;
    else
      long_lose -= ret_val ;
  }

  if (xwork[i] < low_thresh[icomp]) {        // Take a short position?
    if (ret_val < 0.0)
      short_win -= ret_val ;
    else
      short_lose += ret_val ;
  }
} // For training set

criters[icomp] = (long_win + short_win) / (long_lose + short_lose) ;
} // For all competitors
```

All that's left to do is print the sorted criteria. Note how we need to use **sort_key** to recover the competitors' lookahea (holding period) after sorting. My SUP3 program also prints a crude text-oriented graph of the criteria before sorting. I won't clutter this presentation with that simple code; you can find it in SUP3.CPP.

```
qsortdsi ( 0 , n_looks-1 , criters , sort_key ) ;

for (icomp=n_looks-1 ; icomp>=0 ; icomp--) { // Best to worst
  k = sort_key[icomp] ;
  // Print look_low + k, criters[icomp], counts[icomp]
  }
```

Demonstrating the SUP3 Program

I ran the SUP3 program on OEX from early 1988 through 2019. The indicator was PRICE INTENSITY with a smoothing lookback of 3. Holding periods ranged from 1 through 20. Trend elimination took place, and I used 1,000 replications. The following sorted criteria and their associated failure rates were obtained:

Parameter	Profit factor	p-value
8	1.486	0.129
7	1.461	0.095
9	1.445	0.090
5	1.443	0.087
6	1.438	0.130
3	1.415	0.162
4	1.406	0.187
1	1.378	0.254
2	1.362	0.305
10	1.054	0.452
11	1.012	0.614
15	0.996	0.728
14	0.987	0.775
18	0.985	0.822
19	0.970	0.817
16	0.967	0.819
17	0.964	0.846
12	0.956	0.892
20	0.948	0.904
13	0.934	0.892

It's clear that the optimal holding period is around 8 bars, although the failure rates are not small enough be be dramatic. My conclusion is that holding periods in that vicinity are likely superior to longer holding periods, although no single holding period stands out as clearly superior to others. This should not be surprising, as if 8 is optimal, 7 and 9 should also be good holding periods. And we also see that the failure rates for longer holding periods are enormous, making it abundantly clear that long holding periods are out of the question. This is displayed on the next page.

Note the seeming anomaly of the failure rate for the best holding period exceeding that of the next few. This is partly due to the test being based on random numbers, but mostly it is due to the same small anti-predictability effect mentioned earlier and common in superiority tests with *small* true predictability. Any *significantly* superior competitor will stand out.

The crude graph shown below was produced by the SUP3 program for this example. It shows a typical pattern for a good indicator or predictive model. The profit factor starts out fairly high with a one-bar holding period, slowly increases to a peak at the optimal holding period, and then tapers off to small and essentially random values as we pass optimality. I have no ready explanation for why the dropoff after the peak is so rapid, but I see this often.

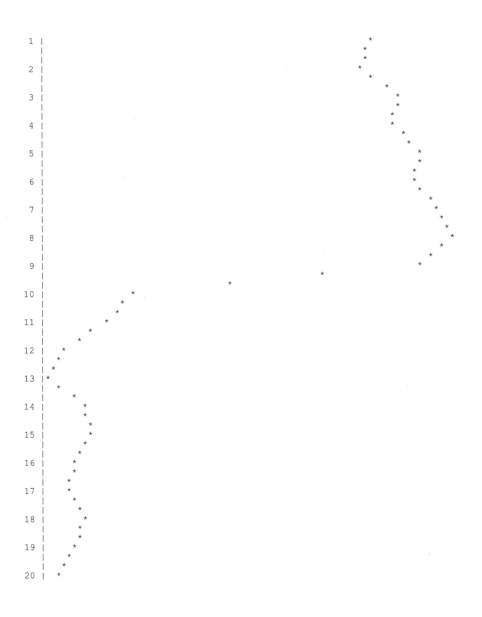

Index

www.ingramcontent.com/pod-product-compliance
Lightning Source LLC
LaVergne TN
LVHW081343050326
832903LV00024B/1294